WHAT IS KARMA?

...the term karma in its original reference includes mental actions. Karma is simply a power of the Universal Mind to effect adjustment, to restore equilibrium, and to bring about compensatory balance. In the sphere of human conduct the result is that somehow, somewhere and somewhen, whatever we do is ultimately reflected back to us. No deed is exhausted in the doing of it; eventually it will bear fruit which will return inexorable to the doer. Karma is a self-moving force. Nobody, human or superhuman, has to operate it.

WHAT IS KARMA?

PAUL BRUNTON

New Age Books

ISBN: 978-81-7822-331-5

First Indian Edition: Delhi, 2009

Originally published in English in USA.

This edition published by arrangement with Paul Brunton Philosophic Foundation 4936 NYS Route 414, Burdett, NY 14818 USA

Published by
NEW AGE BOOKS
A-44 Naraina Phase-I
New Delhi-110 028 (INDIA)
Email: nab@vsnl.in
Website: www.newagebooksindia.com

For Sale in South-East Asia Only

Printed in India
at Shri Jainendra Press
A-45 Naraina Phase-I, New Delhi-110 028

CONTENTS

Introduction 7

1 What Karma Is 15

2 How Karma Works 28
Karma and inner evolution
Learning by doing
Freedom, fate, destiny
Freedom and environment
Group karma
Karma and foreknowledge
Timing, cycles, intensity
Individual accountability

3 Karma and Grace 81
The wonder of grace
Recognizing grace
Invoking grace

4 Working with Karma 102
Apply your understanding
Counter harmful tendencies
Accept, endure, overcome

5 Karma and the Great Liberation 132
Beyond personal karma

Paul Brunton

INTRODUCTION

"KARMA." A household word by now. Often spoken with whimsy or heard with scorn in intelligent circles. Especially by energetic self-actualizers, who associate it with passivity or hear it as an excuse for laziness or fear of responsibility. Sometimes sighed in real or affected resignation to "God's will."

Imagine my surprise to learn that karma is, in fact, all about self-actualizing. About power and results. That to think of it as a power external to myself is to misunderstand it completely. That to explore how it works is to expand the scope and explore the limits of self-actualization.

Each of us has inner power and a measure of freedom, these teachings say. The consequences of how we choose to use—or choose not to use—that power echo through our lives. The echoes become increasingly complex as life goes on.

Similar choices made again and again become tendencies. Tendencies become habits. Habitual thoughts, habitual emotions, habitual actions take over, color and shape our whole version of the world. We may start thinking that the way things seem to be is the way they really are and have to be. When thinking that way becomes a habit, we can most benefit from understanding the natural law of karma.

The teachings on karma are *not* about dumbly resigning yourself to things as they seem to be. They're about reawakening to your own power to see more clearly and to act more profoundly and effectively. If I can master the force that creates and alters habits, they tell me, I align myself with the force that creates and transforms the world.

Understanding how karma works doesn't lead to simply enlightened selfishness. It involves much more than just getting savvy about how to become immune from harm and preserve or further your ego's self-interest. Most importantly, and most emphatically, it's not about hiding out—concealing what little you have so things don't get even worse.

Understanding karma takes us out of our inner isolation and beyond issues of pain avoidance and self-preservation. Not only is each of us self-actualizing in the sense of eventually reaping what we sow. The entire universe, we learn from the teachings about karma, is a self-actuating system; its continuous existence and continuous activity depends, like our own, on something infinitely greater than itself in which it is rooted. The entire system gains, loses, or stays the same through what each of its members does or neglects to do. Karma ultimately is our guarantee of meaningful participation in the life of the whole. For better or worse.

These teachings are only secondarily about consequences—only secondarily about why we reap what we do, why our lives have taken the shape they have. They're first about causes, about power, and about inspiring us to exercise our real freedom and *sow* what we would reap, to make *ourselves* into what we think the world needs more of: kindness for kindness, opportunity for opportunity, or whatever we would see more of in the world. They're less about "Vengeance is mine saith the lord" for your failures (though they are about that) than about "You learn and grow by doing" for your efforts.

Your ship will never come in if you don't send one out. To live in a better world, we each have to do our share in bringing it about. So these teachings are about willed actions long before the results of those actions. And before that, about the thoughts and emotions we dwell with that lead to those actions.

Paul Brunton (known to friends and students P.B.) is widely recognized as one of the twentieth century's most perceptive students of ancient wisdom. This little book presents, in condensed and concentrated form, what he learned about karma from a long and richly varied lifetime: from personal research, relentless trial and error, and intimate association with wise men and women from sacred traditions throughout the world. These pithy gems are drawn from a broad span of his writing, ranging from as early as the mid 1940s to shortly before his death in 1981. They concisely present the essence, and many of the details, of the teachings of karma as they appear throughout the world's wisdom traditions.

The esoteric interpretation of karma, he tells us for example, "recognizes that a wholly isolated individual is only a figment of our imagination, that each person's life is intertwined with all humanity's life through ever-expanding circles of local, national, continental, and finally planetary extent; that each thought is influenced by the world's predominant mental atmosphere; and that each action is unconsciously accomplished with the co-operation of the predominant and powerful suggestion given by humanity's general activity. This makes karma the resultant of *all* these mutual associations and consequently raises it from a personal to a collective level. That is to say 'I,' an individual, share in the karma generated by all other individuals, whilst they share in mine. . . . On this larger view karma makes us suffer for and rejoice with society as a whole. Hence we cannot divorce our own welfare from the social welfare. We must escape from inner isolation and join our interests to those of the All-Life. . . . The situation in which we all find ourselves today compels a recognition of this challenging truth in our mutual interest."

Teachings of karma are often developed in relation to teachings about freedom, predestination, grace, and reincarnation. P.B. told me personally in the spring of 1981 that there is no need for anyone to accept reincarnation in order to understand karma, and that what most people say about reincarnation is misleading anyway. I strongly suspect that had he put this little book together himself, he would have edited out most references to reincarnation, so as to present the teachings on karma in the sharpest possible light. I personally am not comfortable in modifying his writings in that way, however, so such references remain as they were written. But readers should bear in mind that P.B. repeatedly emphasized that karma normally actualizes as swiftly as possible.

Another important point: P.B.'s choice of words became increasingly more personal and precise as his understanding deepened through the years. He constantly sought better, clearer ways to say things, ways that break through conventional pat answers and make it easier for readers to get more core meaning with less effort. From early translations of the law of karma as "law of consequences," he moved on to terms such as "law of creative equivalence," "law of recompense," "law of self-responsibility," and so on. Eventually he realized that even the term "law of" could be misleading for people who take that word to imply that karma is a law we can honor or break, choose to obey or disobey. Be aware that, with only a few obvious exceptions, this variety of terms all refers to karma and not some other "law" or principle.

Similarly, his use of the word karma itself evolved throughout his writings. Some speak of karma as the momentum of past actions; others emphasize that it is more meaningful to see it as the power of present acts and intentions. Both are valid: Take the words in context of the particular excerpts in the text that follows.

One personal conversation with P.B. about freedom and predetermination is worth mentioning here, as the idea doesn't emerge as clearly as I would like under its own power in this book. It also brings out something of value about karma.

He said that people who stand for free will are partly right, and so are those who stand for predetermination. Each has something to hear from the other side. When you look at it carefully, he said, life is a highly ordered structure of opportunities. Some of those opportunities are material, some are spiritual. We have no control over the order in which they appear or the time at which they appear; but they are presented to a soul that is free at every moment to choose or refuse the opportunity. Each choice has consequences, and life never presents exactly the same opportunity again.

At any given time, we're living out the consequences of choices made earlier. In that sense, our lives are predetermined in the short run: things already set in motion must generally run their course.

At a deep level, our whole version of the world—and what's possible in it—comes about through the filter of the tendencies we've developed and desires we've strengthened through our own repeated choices.

But we are also free to change the direction of our lives by the way we respond to the next opportunity; so in the long run free will has the day. I wish now that I had thought to ask P.B. what he meant by "short run" and "long run." Was he thinking short term like months or years, or maybe as this lifetime? But there I go again, missing the main point: as fast as possible.

A key element of these teachings is that the best way to appeal against, or to, the principle of karma isn't through prayer but through changing our thoughts. The more we alter the general trend of our thinking for the better, the better our outer life ultimately will become. The choices we make today alter or confirm the direction our life will ultimately go. Karma, far from imprisoning us, actually guarantees our freedom to determine much of what that will be.

That sounds fine when you feel strong, but how about when you don't? What about when you've dug a hole so deep it seems you'll never get out? When things are so bad it seems there's no turning them around? When the momentum of one bad or stupid action creates another and another in an endless and hopeless series? When despair would rob you or your loved ones of any chance for a fresh start or level playing field?

The news is good: the news about the relationship

of karma and grace. Take a look at the note about Jesus and Buddha (page 84), and thumb through chapter three. You may want to read it a few times. It may seem too good to believe. Thank God (literally) it's not.

Finally, what about the very few for whom freedom means something of an entirely different order? The ones not content to think of freedom as a choice between this mansion or that hovel, this ego-centered joy or that ego-centered pain? Those weary of any kind of continued life in the separated ego and longing for the natural state of spirit: a richly textured serenity unruffled by the sorrows joys jubilations horrors or deadly bores of a given day? What does karma mean for them?

Remember the conversation mentioned on page 12? "Some of the opportunities are material, some are spiritual." Choice remains, consequences differ. We learn that even the tendency to identify with the narrow interests of the personal ego is a habit reinforced or weakened by how freely we choose, or refuse, to do it. Chapters four and five give us an idea of what it's like to work at picking the options that free the spirit, exercising all the while the awesome freedom karma guarantees we will eventually use wisely.

PAUL CASH
EDITOR

1 WHAT KARMA IS

It is absurd to treat the idea of karma as if it were some outlandish Oriental fancy. It is simply the law which makes each of us responsible for our own actions and which puts us into the position of having to accept the results which flow from them. We may call it the law of self-responsibility. The fact that it is allied with the theory of reincarnation does not invalidate it, for we may see it at work in our own present incarnation quite often.

The literal meaning of karma is "doing" and the applied meaning is simply that a person's karma is his or her own doing. We have made ourselves what we are now by our own actions—the term karma in its original reference includes mental actions. Karma is simply a power of the Universal Mind to effect adjustment, to restore equilibrium, and to bring about compensatory balance. In the sphere of human conduct the result is that somehow, somewhere and somewhen, whatever we do is ultimately reflected back to us. No deed is exhausted in the doing of it; eventually it will bear fruit which will return inexorably to the doer. Karma is a self-moving force. Nobody, human or superhuman, has to operate it.

This teaching does not turn us into lethargic fatalists as it does not permit us to swell into conceited individualists. It neither offers any excuse for a miserable weakness, nor bolsters up an illusory strength. It does inspire us with a balanced view of our possibilities, a sane view of our powers.

The materialists paint a terrible picture of the universe as a vast prison where our fate, thoughts, and acts are wholly determined by our physical environment. The ignorant among Orientals live in a locked-up world where we pace helplessly to and fro —prisoners of divine predestination. Karma refutes both these dreary contentions and assigns us sufficient freedom to shape ourselves and our surroundings. By our own development we effect or enrich our environment, help or hinder Nature, and the reverse is also true. Karma does not say that we must stand waiting like ragged beggars before the door of fate. Our past free will is the source of our present fate, as our present one will be the source of our future fate. Consequently the most powerful factor of the two is our own will. There is therefore no room either for foggy fatalism or over-confidence. None of us can escape personal responsibility in the matter of shaping our own internal outlook and external environment by laying the blame on something or someone else. Everyone who is struggling with obstacles should drink a cup of the wine of inspiration from the hand of Beethoven—master music-maker. He who sought to hear the elfin strains of music was himself struck stone deaf. He whose life was completely dedicated to melodious composition for others one day became unable to hear his own compositions. It disappointed but did not discourage him. Facing this problem with a stout heart, he declared, "I will grapple with Fate; it shall never drag me down!" He went on with his work and gave still greater and grander things to the world, for what he learned in suffering he taught in song.

Karma is a twofold law, one being general and the other special. The first is ultimate, and applicable to everything in the universe for it is simply the law of every individual entity's own continuity. Whether it be a planet or a protoplasm it has to inherit the characteristics of its own previous existence and thus adjust effect to cause. The second is immediate, and applicable only to individuals who have attained self-consciousness, thus limiting the start of its operations to human entities. This makes the individual accountable for thoughts and for the deeds born of his or her thoughts.

The universe could not exist as such if there were not some sort of equilibrium holding it together, some sort of balancing arrangement as in the spinning of the earth on its axis and the planets around the sun. A little thought will show the same principle in the just relation of human beings to the World-Mind [God] and among themselves. Here it appears as karma.

It would be an error to separate karma from the universal power and to treat it as an independent power. This error accounts for the difficulty in understanding its role in bringing the cosmos into manifestations. Treat karma rather as an aspect of God and as inseparable from God, or as one of the ways in which God's presence manifests itself.

The real nature of karma is not grasped if it is believed to be a power external to the self, ruthlessly dictating its decrees for our helpless submission. On the contrary, by virtue of the fact that the whole world is mental it is a power working in everything and everyone. This yields the clear implication that what happens to us happens by the secret will of our own innermost being. From this standpoint the sufferings we may have to endure are not evils in the ultimate but only in the immediate sense and what appears as a blind external and ruthless force is really a conscious internal and purifying one.

The correct meaning of the word "karma" is willed action through body, speech, and mind. It does not include the results of this action, especially those which produce or influence rebirth. Such inclusion has come into popular concepts, but shows a loose use of the term. Karma is cause set going by the will, not effect at all. The phrase "Law of Recompense" is therefore not satisfactory and a better one is needed.

The law of recompense may possibly be better named the law of reflection. This is because every act is reflected back to its doer, every thought is reflected back to its source, as if by a vast cosmic mirror. Perhaps the idea of recompense carries too strong a moral implication and hence too limited a meaning to be the correct equivalent for the word "karma."

The law of consequences is not primarily an ethical law: more properly it may be said to have an ethical side.

It is incorrect and unscientific to speak of a "law" of karma. Karma is not a law to obey or disobey, nor is it a penal code for wrong-doers. It is simply the principle of inevitable consequences.

Karma in the sphere of human conduct is neither more nor less than character. We really have as much free will as we need. If we do not avail ourselves of proffered opportunities because we are too blind to recognize them, the fault lies in ourselves. If we embark on an action which is initially and superficially profitable, but ultimately and profoundly inimical to our own interests, and it brings in its train a whole line of other undesirable actions as the sequence, we should not weep at karma's cruelty but at our own lack of intelligence. Those who practice self-pity as a habit may find a convenient scapegoat in karma, but the truth is that the ethical standards and mental qualities of humanity are the hidden factors which predetermine our fate. Karma is not an idea which need dull our minds or paralyze our hands. It has a positive value and a regenerating influence by awakening both in nations and in individuals a sense of ethical responsibility, thus inducing them to heal voluntarily the wounds caused by past errors.

The ethics of former centuries were founded on uncertain fears of a probably existent God; the ethics of the present are founded on complete indifference to a non-existent God. The first led to some restraint on conduct, and the second leads to none. The ethics of the future will be founded on rational understanding of the power of karma, the law of personal responsibility; and this will lead to right restraint on conduct. For when we contemplate the environmental limitations of life, the unsought pleasures and inescapable hardships, we come quietly into a perception of the power of karma.

In karma we find a key to many puzzles of contemporary history. It is a doctrine which warns us that we have prepared the cocoon of our present lot largely by the thoughts and deeds spun out of ourselves during bygone earth-lives and the present reembodiment. Now the doctrine is as applicable to the history of whole peoples as to the history of single individuals. Its corollary is that our characters and minds are in travail through the ages; some are old with the rich experience of a hoary past but most are young, unwise, and ungoverned. Its lesson is that the changing tides of public fate and private fortune are not meaningless. On the contrary, they invite our philosophical consideration so that we may understand how neglected duties or positive wrong-doing are the hidden root of our troubles. Those who understand the principle of karma aright, who do not misunderstand it as being an external independent fate but see it as a force originally set in motion by our actions, understand also the significant part played by suffering in human life. It is educative rather than retributive. Merited punishment is really a crude form of education. Thoughtful people learn lessons from their sorrows and resolve not to commit the same sin or the same error a second time.

Karma, being made by human will, is subject to human modification. Fate, being decreed by the higher power, is not. The general fact of death is an example of fate, and in this sense the poet James Shirley's line: "There is no armour against Fate," is true. But the particular fact of death, its time and manner, may be alterable.

If it be true that the course of life is predetermined, this does not necessarily mean that it is arbitrarily predetermined. No—the good and bad qualities of your character, the development or lack of development of your capacities, and the decisions made in passing or by reason are the real determinants of your life. There is an inescapable equation between conduct and consequence, between thought and environment, between character and destiny. And this is karma, the law of creative equivalence.

The processes of imagining are endless and incessant. It is inherent in mind that one idea should give rise to another because of the dynamic character of mind itself. Karma is the law that links the two.

Karma has a twofold character. There is the kind which nothing that human wit may devise can alter, and there is also the kind which we may alter by counter-thoughts and counter-actions, or by repentance and prayer. Evil karma cannot be extinguished without moral repentance, although it may be modified by astuteness.

There is a large and decided factor between the original meaning of karma and that which has come to be assigned to it through the efflux of time. . . . For whereas karma has come to mean that people's lives are predestined and patterned for them all the way from conception before birth to cremation after death, its original meaning was simply that one could not escape from the consequences of his or her habitual thoughts and acts. It meant that success or failure in life lays largely in our own hands, that satisfaction or sorrow follows inevitably upon the heels of virtue or wrong-doing.

The ability or cupidity, the opportunity or inheritance, which brings someone into the possession of riches, is itself the product of that individual's karma.

The present comes to us out of the past and the future is being made in the present. All three are linked together. . . . This is one of the oldest ideas to be found in human culture, this idea that human life is subject to a higher power, that each of us is personally responsible to a higher law for our actions and that we cannot escape its retribution for wrongdoing or its reward for righteousness. The Stoics of ancient Rome had this idea and called it Fate. The Platonists of ancient Greece had it and called it Destiny. And the Indians, mostly Buddhists and Hindus, had it and have it and call it Karma.

When the revelation of the World-Idea came to religious mystics they could only call it "God's Will." When it came to the Greeks they called it "Necessity." The Indians called it "Karma." When its echoes were heard by scientific thinkers they called it "the laws of Nature."

Anyone with an eye to see can see that the universe reveals that it is being held in intelligent and intelligible order. Arbitrary caprice did not create the world once upon a time. Blind disorder has not ruled it since then. There is true meaning, there is strict law, there is genuine coherence, there is a movement through stone to flower, through beast to human, through higher and higher levels of integration in this universal existence. When this is understood, it can then also be understood that karma is not merely a law of inheriting previous impressions or of self-reproduction or of moral retributive justice but is also something much larger. It is an eternal law which tends to adjust the individual operation to the universal operation. It works for the universe as a whole to keep its innumerable units in harmony with its own integral balance. Retribution merely falls inside this activity as a small concentric circle falls inside a larger one. The results of each individual's existence, each person's heritage of thought and action, have to be controlled so that they shall in the end obey the larger regularity of the cosmos itself. Every part is bound to the whole. Everything thus tends to ultimate rightness. It is indeed comforting to perceive that the universe has such significant equilibrium at its secret core.

The esoteric interpretation of karma recognizes that a wholly isolated individual is only a figment of our imagination, that each individual's life is intertwined with all humanity's life through ever-expanding circles of local, national, continental, and finally planetary extent; that each thought is influenced by the world's predominant mental atmosphere; and that each action is unconsciously accomplished with the co-operation of the predominant and powerful suggestion given by humanity's general activity. The consequences of what each of us thinks and does flows like a tributary into the larger river of society and there mingle with waters from innumerable other sources. This makes karma the resultant of *all* these mutual associations and consequently raises it from a personal to a collective level. That is to say "I," an individual, share in the karma generated by all other individuals, whilst they share in mine. There is a difference, however, between both our shares in that "I" receive the *largest* share of the results of my own personal past activity and that the smallest share of the results of the rest of humanity's activity.

Hence our hint that not all sufferings are merited ones but that compensatory good fortune comes accordingly into play. If owing to humanity's interdependence we have to suffer what we have not personally earned, it is equally true that owing to the same interdependence we are able to receive unearned benefits from the general good karma. Thus this collective operation of karma is like a two-edged sword which cuts both ways: the one painful and the other enjoyable. The esoteric view puts a fresh face on the popular form of the doctrine, and if it has generally been kept in the background this is only because people are more interested in their own personal welfare than in the common welfare. . . .

We live in common with others, sin in common too and must be redeemed in common. This is the last word, dismaying perhaps to those who have outstripped their fellows but heartening to those who have lagged behind. On this larger view karma makes us suffer for and rejoice with society as a whole. Hence we cannot divorce our own welfare from the social welfare. We must escape the inner isolation and join our interests to the All-Life. There is no need for antagonism between classes, nations, and races, no need for hatred and strife between different groups whether large or small. All are ultimately interdependent. Their separateness is as great a delusion as separateness of individuals, but only philosophy and history prove this truth. The situation in which we all find ourselves today compels a recognition of this challenging truth in our mutual interest.

2 HOW KARMA WORKS

There is no supernatural and external being who arbitrarily administers or controls karmic rewards or punishments. We unconsciously produce their seeds ourselves; when a favorable hour comes, they germinate and yield their own fruit.

It is not that some mysterious superphysical angel, deva, or god intervenes personally and manipulates karma as a puppet performer pulls the wires of his suspended figures, but that karma is part of the equilibrium of the universe, bringing a come-back, recording a pressure, allowing each reaction to come about by its own momentum.

The working of karma traces complicated effects back to complicated causes.

If in the end—and sometimes well before—karma

catches up with you, it is not all painful; the term need not fill you with foreboding. For the good you have thought and done brings a good come-back too.

No human existence is without its troubles at some period or without its frictions at another. The first arises out of the element of destiny which surrounds human freedom, the second out of the element of egoism which surrounds human relations.

Through its ignorance of karmic operations and effects, the ego provokes many of its own oppositions and much of its own troubles.

We invite the future through our aspirations. We get the consequences of our thinking, feeling, and doing. Nature has no favoritism but gives us our deserts.

Although karma is clinched by what a person does in fact, it is built up also by what he or she long thinks and strongly feels.

When at length you will be called to account by karma, you will be judged not by the certificates of character which others bestow upon you, whether good or bad, but by the motives felt in your heart, the attitudes held in your mind, and the deeds done by your hands.

The law of compensation does *not* measure its rewards and penalties according to the little scale of little human minds.

The utmost use of the reasoning faculties cannot always provide for every factor in a situation. There are some which only intuition can grasp—the karmic factor, for instance. This explains the miscalculations of people who possess the most highly developed rationality but who lack a counterbalancing development of intuition.

Events and environments are attracted to you partly according to what you are and do (individual karma), partly according to what you need and seek (evolution), and partly according to what the society, race, or nation of which you are a member is, does, needs, and seeks (collective karma).

There is a spiritual penalty to pay for every intellectual misbehavior and every moral misconduct, whether there be a worldly penalty or not. For the one, there is the failure to know truth; for the other, there is the failure to find happiness.

Karma expresses itself through events which may seem to be accidents. But they are so only on the surface.

Things act according to their nature. The World-Idea records these actions in a secret way and reflects back their appropriate results. And as with things so with persons. Each of us sings a note out into the universe, and the universe answers us in the same key.

Karma gives you what you have largely made yourself; it does not give you what you prefer: but it is quite possible at times that the two coincide. If you are partially the author of your own troubles, you are also drawing to yourself by mental power your good fortune.

If your destiny—the fragment of fate apportioned to you—desires you to achieve a certain task, a particular mission, then—however much you may dally in secluded retreat—it will provide you with an inner compulsion that at the appointed hour will drag you from retirement into the public arena again. Even if the task has been distant from your desire and concealed from your conscious mind during all previous years, you will still have to obey this unexpected inner force, this overwhelming bidding which is but the voice of destiny making itself heard in this way. Yes, paradoxically one carries one's fate within one's self. Karma needs to send no attorney to plead its cause.

Forces out of your own reincarnatory past come up and push you towards certain decisions, actions, and attitudes.

Ouspensky's theory of eternal recurrence is both true and false. We repeat ourselves and our circumstances but always on a different level. It is a spiral not a circle. An event or a period in life corresponds to a previous one but is not identical with it. The future is analogous with the past but does not duplicate it. The spiral does not bring you back identically the same self or the same work: it brings you to what corresponds to it on a different level.

Our outward miseries are symbols and symptoms of our inner failures. For every self-created suffering and every self-accepted evil is an avoidable one. It may not depend entirely upon yourself how far events can hurt you but it does depend largely upon yourself. If you had the strength to crush your egoism by a single blow, and the insight to penetrate the screen of a long series of causes and effects, you would discover that half your external troubles derive from faults and weaknesses of internal character. Every time you manifest the lower attributes of your internal character you invite their reflection in external events. Your anger, envy, and resentment will, if strong enough and sustained enough, be followed eventually by troubles, enmities, frictions, losses, and disappointments.

There are no lucky house-numbers and no unlucky ones. If you have had a series of misfortunes in a certain house, it is not the fault of its number but the fault of your karma. Your evil karma fell due during that period and would have ripened into sorrowful experiences even if you had occupied a totally different house with a totally different number. Now karma arises ultimately out of character for the better and thus ultimately changes your karma to some extent. Then move back into the same house which once brought you sorrow. You will find that this time it will not do so. Its so-called unlucky number will no longer harm you.

All the karmic tendencies are not present in consciousness at the same time; some have yet to pass from the potential to the kinetic condition.

People should be warned that cause and effect rule in the moral realm no less than in the scientific realm. They should be trained from childhood to take this principle into their calculation. They should be made to feel responsible for setting causes into action that invite suffering or attract trouble or lead to frustration.

There is an inescapable balance between our principal thoughts and deeds and our principal life experiences. And this balance shows itself where it is least expected—in the moral sphere. Our wrong-doing produces sorrows, not only for others but principally for ourselves. Our good action produces a rebound of good fortune. We may not escape from the operation of this subtle law of moral responsibility. Causation is the top of a wheel whose bottom is consequence. This is just as true collectively as individually. When, for instance, a nation comes to believe that the conception of right and wrong is a false one, it marks itself down for destruction. We have seen this in our time in the case of the German nation. The moral law is not a figment of human imagination. It is a divinely established reality.

The moral fallacy which leads a people to think that they can build their own happiness out of the misery of other people, can be shattered only by a knowledge of the truth of karma.

Thought tends to be creative and sooner or later it produces karmic fruit in your general environment. This is also true of your moral life. Here, it is not always necessary for your thoughts to translate themselves into deeds before they can become karmically effective. If they have sufficient intensity and if they are prolonged over a sufficient period they will eventually bring appropriate results even in external circumstances. This can be made clearer by an actual illustration. If you persistently wish a person's death, but even if through fear of the consequences you lack the courage to slay the other person, then your murderous thoughts will one day react upon you in an equilibrated form. You may then yourself suffer a violent death or fall victim to a fatal accident or suffer from a disease which is as corrosive to your body as your hatred was to your character. Thus although not actually guilty of committing murder, you undergo a physical penalty for *thinking* murder.

For similar reasons, diseased habits of thinking may manifest themselves as diseased conditions of the flesh. The physician may rightly see the immediate physical cause of such a condition but may not see the ultimate mental one, which may be excessive anger, morbid hate, overpowering fear, inordinate lust, or habitual spite. We must not, of course, leap to the illogical conclusion that everyone who suffers from a disease has been thinking negatively in the past or present. The body has its own hygienic laws which cannot be transgressed with impunity, although most transgressions usually occur through sheer ignorance.

All this is possible because the entire basis of existence is a mentalist one. The creative factor in the karmic process is the mind itself. Consequently a mental change is needful if its operation against us is to be radically and favorably altered.

What rich, envied family is there which is without a skeleton of suffering or misfortune in its cupboard? Who does not know of some who have two or three skeletons? You may have found, as so many have done in these dark days, that life contains mysterious and potent karmic influences which reach out ominous hands to break the things you have set your heart upon; which permit you to achieve success and then destroy it before your eyes; which play havoc with the health and perhaps the lives of those near and dear to you. Your heart may have bled in silence.

We create our own burdens of latent suffering when our deeds injure others, and we give birth to bitter ultimate consequences when we give birth to thoughts of hatred. The forces of lust, greed, and anger are blind ones which uncontrolled, unleashed, and unguided lead humanity to so much karmic trouble and misery.

A fire may be used to roast food or to roast someone at the stake. The fire itself is not an evil, but the use or abuse of it is good or evil; and this in its turn depends on what impulses are working in a person's heart, what tendencies that person has brought over from past lives. Thus evil powers are after all our own evil thoughts. The world will be liberated from evil as soon as people liberate their mind. Mind is the agent whereby the working of karma is effected. There is no need to call in an extra-cosmic supernatural being to explain how deeds are requited.

The law of recompense is not the only one to compel us to right thought, feeling, and conduct. On a higher plane, there is the Overself. Were there no rewards for goodness and no punishment for wickedness, either here on earth or somewhere in a death-world, it would still be a part of our highest happiness to express the compassion that is, through the Overself, our purest attribute.

Your own actions will in turn lead to someone else's further actions.

Human instruments *are* used to cause suffering to others and they *do* cause it out of human viciousness. Both statements are correct. They are complementary, not contradictory as we may think. Destiny naturally looks around for a vicious person when she wants to do harm, or a foolish one who can be led emotionally by the nose for a time, or an impulsive one who may do in a moment what he regrets for years. She will not waste time looking for ultra-wise and ultra-good people when she wants to do harm.

A life that is not directed towards this higher goal, a mind that is entirely uninterested in becoming a participant in the Overself consciousness—these failures silently censure people both during their bodily tenancy and their post-mortem existence.

Sins of omission are just as important karmically as sins of commission. What we ought to have done but did not do counts also as a karma-maker.

Even deliberate inaction does not escape the making of a karmic consequence. It contains a hidden decision *not* to act and is therefore a form of action!

The attempt to evade karma may itself be part of the karma.

The study of recompense (karma) reveals that people have to pay not only for what they have wrongly done but also for what they have failed to do. Such neglect is largely due to this, that people's intensely personal outlook makes them estimate the character of events primarily by the way in which they affect their own existence and only secondarily by the way in which they affect the larger human family to which they belong. We are all workers in a common task. This is the inevitable conclusion which shares itself as soon as the truth of humanity as an organic unity is understood.

There is a clear duty in this inner-dependent age to *help* actively on the right side. The world distress is mostly due to karma. But we need a broader interpretation of this word. Many of us may be good and innocent but we have to suffer with all others, not for what we have done but for what we left undone. Today sorrow misses nobody. This is because humanity is completely interdependent. That is the lesson we have to learn; that we let others remain in woe or ignorance at our own peril. We are one.

The collective karmic impressions rise of themselves within the World-Mind. This is because there has never been a time when they did not exist for, although their forms may change, they are as eternal as the World-Mind itself. Indeed, they are part of the World-Mind's nature. Hence they constitute a self-actuating system. Because we can set no date for the World-Mind's own beginning nor any terminus for its own life, we must consequently refrain from the illogical attempt to set a beginning or an end to the universe itself. And the World-Mind has not *made* the world but only afforded the ground for its existence, the receptacle for its mutually acting karmic potential forces, the stuff for its general karmic manifestations, and the life-principle for its ever-moving activities which take place of their own accord. But we must not fall into the error that this view makes the universe a mere machine. For the ground receptacle forces and stuff all being mental, the world also is a mental activity and not just a mechanical movement in matter.

The mysterious working of karma, this force which molds the conditions of every center of being from protoplasmic cell to vast cosmos, must next be uncovered. If the world were nothing but a collection of material objects, karma could never come into play. But because it is, as mentalism shows, a collection of thought-formations and because there is a World-Mind as the unitary ground connecting all these formations, the possibility of karma as an operative force exists. For karma would be meaningless if there were not some kind of orderly continuity between the past, the present, and the future of all those things and creatures which make up the universal existence. But this implies that Nature must keep and conserve some sort of memory in her secret recesses.

If every individual preserves a record of his own history, why should it seem fantastic for the World-Mind to preserve a record of its own history? And because its existence is inseparable from the manifested cosmos, in doing this it preserves an all-comprehensive record of the universe's own history too. No thought, no event, no object, no scene, and no figure has ever been wholly lost. This implies that the memories of globes and stars and nebulae utterly remote in space and time are still preserved. But human imagination must stagger away from the boundless consequences of this truth, its finite limitations here defeating its own activity. And because memory is not an object which the senses can grasp but something entirely immaterial, this in turn involves the existence of something mental. A mental principle which shall be cosmic in its spatial sweep and permanent in its embrace of time, is and can be none other than the World-Mind itself. Thus the foundation of all karmic working can be traced to the World-Mind. The rise, abiding, and dissolution of karma is indeed a twin-function to that of its ideation.

One and the same light refracts itself into a million photographs, each different from all others. One and the same World-Mind refracts itself into a million persons, each different from all others. And just as the objects in the universe come into existence by the power of karma, so do the individuals too. The new creature emerges into the universal existence in much the same way as the new thing, that is through an actualization of the train of its old karmic impressions which are themselves the resultant of a still earlier existence. The individual and the world rise together at the same moment out of the past which trails behind both. Its karmas are associated with those of the universal existence and do not appear separately or subsequently. The one starts into activity synchronously with the stirring of the other. When the World-Mind's energy manifests itself it takes a twofold character and both the universe and the individuals are born at the same time. The universe is not manifested first nor the individuals either but both together. To put it another way, as the ripples of karma flow across the lake of World-Mind they move through both the universe and the individual at the same instant and, operationally, in the same way.

Karma, being the kinetic memory of Nature, is necessarily coupled with the imaginative power of Nature.

Just as a massive oak tree once had an invisible and intangible existence in the acorn or the gentle fragrance of a white flower once had an unsmelled existence in the tiny seed, so the earth and stars and sun which we see around us today once had an immaterial existence in the germinal form which their own karma had stored within the memory of the World-Mind. Every starry body in the firmament with its particular distinguishing characteristics and every creature which dwelt upon it with its own desires, tendencies, and capacities were memorized by the wonderful faculties of World-Mind. From this it will be seen that memory played a potent part in creating the world of which we are conscious.

It is through mutually-acting karmic processes that this universe become possible. The World-Mind brings forth its general world-images not by any arbitrary fiat but by their natural continuity as the consequences of all those that have previously existed. They are a continuation of all the remembered world-images which have appeared before, but modified and developed by their own mutual interaction and evolution, not by the capricious decree of a humanized God. The World-Mind makes the universe by constructively thinking it. But it does not think arbitrarily. The thoughts rise of their own accord under a strict karmic and evolutionary law. It must be emphasized that on this view the universe constitutes a self-actuating system, although it must equally be understood that the system itself depends on World-Mind for its own continued existence and continuous activity. All the karmic forces and thought-forms carry on their mutual activities, intertwine, interact and evolve of their own accord in the presence of sunlight. But it is to that very presence that they owe their own sustenance and existence.

Karma and inner evolution

While fulfilling its own purpose, karma cannot help fulfilling another and higher one; it brings us what is essential to our development.

Events happening to us are not necessarily karmic in the sense that we earned them. They can also have a non-karmic source. No physical doing on our part brought them on, but they are what we need at that point for character or capacity, development or correction. Both kinds are fated. In that sense they are God's will.

The human will's freedom has its limits. It must in the end conform to the evolutionary purposes of the World-Idea. If, by a certain time, it fails to do so voluntarily, then these purposes invoke the forces of suffering and force the human entity to conform.

There are times when, for your inner evolution, your ego has to be crushed, and you may then find yourself bent under harsh events or melancholy reflections.

If your evolutionary need should require it, you will be harassed by troubles to make you less attached to the world, or by sickness to make you less attached to the body. It is then not so much a matter of receiving self-earned destiny as of satisfying that need. Both coincide usually but not always and not necessarily. Nor does this happen with the ordinary person so much as it does with people on the spiritual quest, for the latter have asked or prayed for speedier development.

Are some faults of conduct, weaknesses of character, quite incorrigible? Give yourself enough time, that is to say, enough lifetimes, and you will be unable to resist change and reform, that is to say, unable to resist the World-Idea. God is will in religious parlance.

Learning by doing

Life is not trying to make people either happy or unhappy. It is trying to make them understand. Their happiness or unhappiness come as by-products of their success or failure in understanding.

I believe in love, not hate, as a motivating force for reform. At the same time, I see karma at work, punishing the selfish and the heartless, and I know that it will inexorably do its work whatever anyone says. God never makes a mistake and this universe is run on perfect laws. Unfortunately, suffering is one of its chief instruments of evolution and especially so where people will not learn from intuition, reason, and spiritual prophets.

People who artfully hurt others in the end hurt themselves. For they deny the principle of love in their relationships, a principle that is part of the higher laws set for our development, and must pay the penalty of their denial.

Karma is really neutral although to the human observer its operations seem to be rewarding or punitive.

We do not endure certain troubles or disappointing experiences during life without a particular reason for each one. If we take the trouble to learn the reason we can conquer the experience and strengthen our character, or we can permit the experience to conquer us and to worsen our character. Through many and widely varied experiences we are given opportunity to build our capacities of thought and judgment, will and intuition. Experiences rightly handled can become effective means for our passing from a lower to a higher standpoint. Every experience should be exploited for its lessons, whether it be painful or pleasurable, as a novelist might exploit it for story material.

When we know the results of our actions, we have the chance to know the value of those ideas which led to these actions. In other words, experience will bring responsibility, if we allow it to, and that will bring development.

Fate is fashioned in such a way that it gives people at times what they want, so that they shall eventually, through this experience, learn to evaluate it more justly. They have then the opportunity to see the adverse side of the experience, which desire too often prevents them from seeing. Fate is also fashioned to go into reverse and block the fulfillment of the wishes of other people. Through this inhibition they may have the chance to learn that we are not here for a narrow, egoistic satisfaction alone, but also, and primarily, to fulfill the larger purposes of life as formed in the World-Idea.

Cults which teach that destiny either does not matter or is non-existent are cults which can never lead to true happiness, for they illustrate that blind leading of the blind of which we have heard before. Destiny exists, and it is wise to face and acknowledge the fact. The mere refusal to acknowledge its existence does not thereby limit it. It is there and no amount of prayer or concentration will dismiss it because it exists for the benefit of humanity—for our ethical and intellectual education—and because while living in this world we cannot have one without the other.

When rendering an account of good or bad fortune, people usually forget to include the ethical values which were acquired from each experience. But when we have attained some understanding of such matters, we will involuntarily bring the truth of personal responsibility into this light, not merely as an intellectual dogma but as a heartfelt conviction.

The law of recompense is not nullified nor proved untrue by the objector's proffered evidence of hard ruthless individuals who rose to influence and affluence over the crushed lives of other persons. The happiness or well-being of such individuals cannot be properly judged by their bank account alone or their social position alone. Look also into the condition of their physical health, of their mental health, of their conscience in the dream state, of their domestic and family relations. Look, too, into their next reincarnation. Then, and only then, can the law's presence or absence be rightly judged.

We do not easily grow from the worse to the better or from the better to the best. We struggle out of our imperfections at the price of toil sacrifice and trouble. The evil of these things is not only apparent nor, in essence, in any ultimate conflict with divine love. Whatever helps us in the end towards the realization of our diviner nature, even if it be painful, is good and whatever hinders, even if it be pleasant, is bad. If a personal sorrow tends towards this result it is really good and if a personal happiness retards it, then it is really bad. It is because we do not believe this that we complain at the presence of suffering and sorrow in the divine plan and at the absence of mercy in the divine will. We do not know where our true good lies, and blindly following ego, desire, emotion, or passion, displace it by a fancied delusive good. Consequently, we lose faith in God's wisdom at the very time when it is being manifested and we become most bitter about God's indifference just when God's consideration is being most shown to us. Until we summon enough courage to desert our habitual egoistic and unreflective attitude, with the wrong ideas of good and evil, happiness and misery which flow out of it, we shall continue to prolong and multiply our troubles unnecessarily.

Imagine what would happen to a hand accidentally put into a fire if there were no nervous system to provide the owner of the hand with a warning signal of pain. It would be altogether destroyed and its use lost forever. Here the pain of being burnt, severe though it be, would really act as a disguised friend if it persuaded the owner to withdraw his hand from the fire. So far as suffering protects physical life, it possesses a justifiable place in the universal scheme of things. Then what about protecting moral life? Pain fills a place in the present evolutionary stage of our ethical existence which is hardly less and often more useful than that filled by pleasure. But our egoism blinds us to this fact. If it does no more than arouse us from the stupor of understanding into which most of us habitually fall, pain will have done something worthwhile. Plato has even pointed out that it is a misfortune to a man who has deserved punishment to escape it. After all, the punishment may awaken him to the recognition that wrong has been done and thus purify his character. Again, it is through pain that a man's cruelty and pride and lust may be broken, for they are hardly amenable to correction by mere words. The pain inflicted on a swollen sense of "I," for example, by karmic compensatory working is not really punishment any more than is the pain inflicted by a surgeon who opens an abscess with a knife.

When his life does not develop along the line he has planned, his mind will become confused and self-doubt will creep in. It is then that the ambitious man is taken in hand by his higher self, to learn through frustration and disappointment released by the new cycle of bad karma those lessons he could not receive through success and triumph.

The subconscious connection between wrongs done and sufferings incurred leads us to feel more uncertain and more uncomfortable the more we engage in such acts.

A callous egotism is a bad-paying investment. For it means that in time of need, there will be none to help; in the hour of distress, none to console. What we give out we get back.

The brutal egotist who ruthlessly knocks others aside on his way upward will himself receive harsh treatment when the time is decreed.

The deer which lies mortally wounded by a hunter's shot is not capable of asking Life why it should suffer so, but the man who lies mortally wounded by a murderer's shot *is* capable of doing so.

The wheel of life keeps turning and turning through diverse kinds of experiences and we are haplessly bound to it. But when at last we gain comprehension of what is happening and power over it, we are set free.

The iron of human character turns to tempered steel in the white-hot furnace of trouble.

Freedom, fate, destiny

It must not be supposed that we are so helpless as it would seem. Much of our destiny was made by ourselves in the past. We made it, therefore we can help to change it. Destiny controls us, but our free will has some control over destiny. This will be true, however, only to the extent that we learn the lessons of experience and creatively exercise that free will.

We can accept neither the arrogant Western attitude which believes itself to be the master of life nor the hopeless Oriental attitude which believes itself to be the victim of life. The one overvalues human creativeness, the other undervalues it. The one believes it can banish all human ills, the other regards them as irremediable.

When the belief in destiny is allowed to paralyze all energy and overwhelm all courage, it should be re-examined. When the belief in free will is allowed to lead people into egoistic arrogance and materialistic ignorance, it also should be re-examined.

The old arguments about fate and free will are in the end quite useless. It is possible to show that we have the full freedom to improve ourselves and our surroundings, but it is also possible to show that we are helpless. This is so because *both* sides of the matter are present and must be included in any account of the human situation. The World-Idea renders certain events and circumstances inevitable.

If we analyze the meaning of words instead of using them carelessly, we shall find that in this case of "free will" the term often stands for the very opposite idea to that for which it is supposed to stand. Where is the real freedom of people who are enslaved by their appetites and in bondage to their passions? When they express what they believe to be their own will they are in actuality expressing the will of those appetites and passions. So long as desires, passions, environments, heredity, and external suggestions are the real sources of our actions, where is our real free will? Without freedom from desires there is no freedom of will. Unless you find your true self you cannot find your true will. The problem of fate versus free will must first be understood before it can be solved. And this understanding cannot be had whilst we make the usual superficial approach instead of the rarer semantic approach. Our will is free but only relatively so.

There is no complete freedom but, on the other hand, there is no complete necessity. There is a confined free will, a freedom within bounds. Philosophy makes, as the basis of this freedom in humanity, both the intelligence it finds in us and the Divine Spirit from which that intelligence is derived.

The materialist doctrine of "determinism" is a mixture of truth and falsity. It rightly points to the way our outer lives are determined by our outer circumstances and events. It wrongly deprives us of the freedom to react as we choose to those circumstances and events. It is quite untrue where moral choice is concerned.

We may ask if there is any point along our entire course where we really have a choice, really have a chance between two ways, to do what we actually want to do. Our freedom consists in this, that we are free to choose between one act and another but not between the consequences arising out of those acts. We may claim our inner freedom whatever our outer future may be. We may fix our own life aims, choose our own beliefs, form our own ideas, entertain desires, and express aversions as we wish. Here, in this sphere of thought and feeling, action and reaction, free will is largely ours.

The choice between right and wrong can only exist where there is freedom of will to make it. Humans are neither responsible nor free, declares materialistic determinism. If someone is or becomes a criminal, environment is to blame, heredity is to blame, society is to blame—but not the individual. Spiritual determinism, karma (recompense), does not give us so wide a license to commit crime. It asserts that each of us was and is in part the author of our own character, consequently of our own destiny.

When we uphold the existence of free will, we uphold implicitly the existence of fate. For enquiry into the way the thought of freedom arises in the mind reveals that it always comes coupled with the thought of fate. If one is denied, then the other is thereby denied also.

There is a certain amount of destiny in each life as the result of past karma, but there is also an amount of free will if it is exercised. Every happening in our lives is not karmic, for it may be created by our present actions.

Whoever imagines that all his actions are entirely the result of his own personal choice, whoever suffers from the illusion of possessing complete free will, is blinded and infatuated with his ego. He does not see that at certain times it was impossible for him to act in any other way because there was no alternative. And such impossibility arose because there is a law which arranges circumstances or introduces a momentum according to an intelligible pattern. Karma, evolution, and the individual's trend of thought are the principal features of this pattern.

What different course our life might have taken if we had not casually met a certain person—a meeting which led to momentous consequences—affords material for tantalizing speculations. Fate sometimes hangs upon a thread, we are told; but it always hangs upon such a tangled knot of dependent circumstances that the game of speculating how different it would have been had a single one of them been changed, is futile though fascinating.

A person's whole destiny may hang upon one event, one decision, one circumstance. That single cause may be significant for all the years to follow.

Karma's will could not prevail in one special part of our life and not in any other parts, nor in one special event of our life and not in the others. It could not be here but not there, in the past but not now. Nor, going even farther still, could it confine itself only to major items and not to minor ones. It must be ever present or never present at all. If it puts more destiny into the happenings we experience than lets the Westerner feel comfortable, we must remember that other facet of truth, the creative and godlike intelligence in our deeper humanity and the measure of freedom which accompanies it.

The law of recompense has no jurisdiction over the eternal and undivided Overself, the real being, only over the body and mind, the transitory ego.

Those who object to the doctrine of self-determined fate, who put forward an absolute freedom of will, have to show how free will can change the results of a murder. Can it restore life to the corpse or save the criminal from death? Can it remove the unhappiness of the murdered man's wife? Can it even eliminate the sense of guilt from the conscience of his murderer? No—these results inevitably flow from the act.

Overstress of such beliefs as astrology may cause you to understress or even forget entirely your creative possibilities. They are both extreme swings of the pendulum. Astrology rests on the ground of karma in tendencies and deeds. Freedom of decision rests on the evolutionary need to let each person express the creativeness he or she gets from the Overself. You must put both factors together to find truth.

Freedom exists at your heart, that is, in your Overself. Fate exists on your surface-life, that is, in your personality. And as each human being is a compound of both these beings, neither the absolute fatalist nor the absolute free-will position is wholly correct and external life must also be a compound of freedom and fate. . . . No action is entirely free nor entirely fated; all are of this mixed double character.

Heredity, education, experience, karma (both collective and personal), free will, and environment conspire together to fashion both the outer form and inner texture of the life which we have to live. We sew the tapestry of our own destiny but the thread we use is of a kind, a color and quality forced upon us by our own past thoughts and acts. In short, our existence has a semi-independent, semi-predestined character.

Karma brings us the results of our own doing, but these are fitted in the World-Idea, which is the supreme law and shapes the course of things.

Every individual's personal freedom stretches to a certain distance and then finds itself ringed around by fate. Outside this limit he or she is as helpless as a babe, and can do nothing there.

Greek tragic drama shows how event after event may turn against someone at the bidding of a higher power—destiny. It shows how little human will can do to avert catastrophe or avoid disaster when the universal will is set in an opposite direction.

Only so far as personal planning obtains destiny's sanction will it be able to achieve its goals.

What a higher power has decreed must come to pass. But what you have made for yourself you can modify or unmake. The first is fate, the second destiny. The one comes from outside your personal ego, the other from your own faults. The evolutionary will of your soul is part of the nature of things but the consequences of your own actions remain, however slightly, within your own control.

If it were true that every act you did and every event which happened to you was predestined in every point, the destruction of your moral responsibility which would necessarily follow would be as disastrous to society as to yourself.

The web of karma tightens around you as the lives increase with the centuries or thins away as the ego gets more and more detached.

In the somewhat mysterious way whereby fated decree meshes its gear in with willed free choice, the final result appears.

Free will versus Fate is an ancient and useless controversy, which is purely artificial and therefore insoluble as it is ordinarily presented. They are not antinomies but complementaries. They are not in opposition. The wise combine both. In the absence of a knowledge of the factors of karma and evolution, all discussion of such a topic is unreal, superficial, and illusory. As spiritual beings we possess free will; as human beings we do not. This is the key to the whole matter.

You may attempt to defy your destiny, but unless you have emancipated your spirit, it will get you.

What is destined to happen, paradoxically comes to pass through the exercise of our free will.

Freedom and environment

Each of us lives at a certain time in history and occupies a certain place (or certain places) during that period. Why now and here? Look to the law of consequences for an answer, the law which connects one earthly lifetime with earlier ones.

It is quite untrue to say that we are created by our environment. It is true to say that we are conditioned, assisted, or retarded by our environment, but it is only a half-truth. We bear within ourselves a consciousness which, at several points and in different attributes, is independent of and sometimes quite opposed to all environmental suggestions. For, from the first day on earth, we possess in latency certain likes and dislikes, aptitudes along one line of thought and action rather than along others, whose sum, as they disclose themselves and then develop themselves, constitutes our personality. Of course, such a process necessarily takes time. Biological heredity contributes something quite definite toward this result but former incarnations contribute much more.

Surroundings help to bring out a person's innate

qualities or to prevent their manifestation, but they do not create such qualities. If they did, geniuses could be made to order in every school and studio.

The bad environment does not *create* the bad character. It brings it out and encourages its development. The weaknesses were already there latently.

Although it is true that strong or prudent people rule their stars and conquer their circumstances, it is equally true and often overlooked that the strength and the prudence to do so come from within, are born in such people much more than acquired by them.

Average people are not so heroic or so angelic as all that and soon find out that their soul cannot rise above their circumstances and that their nerves are unquestioningly affected by their environment.

You may be predestined to live in certain surroundings but the way in which you allow them to affect you is not predestined.

The people one meets, the events one confronts, and the places one visits may be highly important but they are, in the end, less important than one's thought about them.

Each person who enters our life for a time, or becomes involved with it at some point, is an unwitting channel bringing good or evil, wisdom or foolishness, fortune or calamity to us. This happens because it was preordained to happen—under the law of recompense. But the extent to which they affect our outer affairs is partly determined by the extent to which we let them do so, by the acceptance or rejection of suggestions made by their conduct, speech, or presence. It is we who are finally responsible.

If one person can come up out of the squalor, discomfort, and ignorance of the slums into cleanliness, culture, and refined living, we may read into it either the favorable working of karma and rebirth or the power of that person to conquer environment. But others who fail to do so may read into it the belief that luck is against them or else their lack of capacity to overcome environment. Thus we see that some glean a message of hope from reading the biographies of such people while others glean only frustration, if not despair. In both views there may be an element of truth but how much will differ from one person to another.

The man or woman who is born with a silver spoon may have great talents but never use them. Their talents may die with them, because they never felt the spur of necessity. Insufficient or moderate means may give incentive. The worse the poverty the greater the incentive. This sounds a hard gospel but for some people it is a true one.

Whether you enter birth in penurious squalor or in palatial grandeur, you will come to your own *spiritual* level again in the end. Environment is admittedly powerful to help or hinder, but the Spirit's antecedents are still more powerful and finally *independent of it.*

Group karma

Karma is not merely applicable to the individual alone but also to groups, such as communities, towns, countries, and even continents. One cannot get away in some particular or other from the rest of humanity. All are interconnected. Individuals may delude themselves, as nearly all do, into thinking that they can live their own life and let others go hang, but sooner or later experience reveals their error. All are ultimately *one* big family. This is what reflection on experience teaches. When we reflect on Truth, we shall eventually learn that, as the Overself, all are one entity—like the arms and legs of a single body. The upshot of this is that each of us has to consider the welfare of others equally with our own, not merely because karma is at work to teach the individual, but also because it is at work to teach humanity *en masse* the final and highest lesson of its unity. When this idea is applied to the recent war [WWII], one sees that the latter was partly (only partly) the result of the indifference of richer peoples to poorer ones, of well-governed nations to badly governed ones, of the isolationist feeling that one's country is all right and if others are not, then that is unfortunate but their own affair. In short, there is no true prosperity and happiness for any country while one of its neighbors is poor and miserable; each one is his brother's keeper.

The working of recompense (a piece of karma) also affects those who are closely associated with the person whose own acts or thoughts originated it.

Karma is not and can never be a merely individual matter. Society as a whole creates the slum which creates the criminal. If society calls him to account for his crimes, he may in his turn call society to account for making his criminal character possible. Consequently society must also share with him, if in lesser degree, the karmic responsibility for his misdeeds.

When a whole people move along the road of wrong-doing, then they invite suffering for their purification and enlightenment. So long as selfishness rules society, so long will society have its sufferings. So long as nations are indifferent to the woes of other nations, so long will they themselves sooner or later share those woes. A wealthy people cannot escape a partial responsibility for its refusal to help the poorer peoples, nor a powerful nation for its tolerance of the persecution of others, nor an aggressive race for its forcible domination over weaker races. The world wars have abundantly illustrated these truths.

If we wish to understand what has been happening in the world, we must first understand that continental and national karma are hidden causes of its distresses.

A nation arises by the adding together of every individual in it. You are one of those individuals whose thought and conduct will help to make your nation's karma. The subject of collective destiny is very complicated because it is composed of many more elements than individual destiny. The individual who is born into a particular nation has to share the general destiny of that nation as well as his or her own individual karma. If however they withdraw from that nation by their own choice and migrate to another country, they will then share a new collective destiny which is bound to modify their own and put its mark on it, either improving it by giving them more opportunity or causing it to deteriorate.

There is a collective national karma which gradually grows and then materializes. When a group of people live together and work together, either in a country or a city, they gradually form for themselves a national or a municipal destiny which they have to bear. Sometimes the result is good, sometimes it is bad, but generally it is a mixture of both. Hence we find in history such things as a national destiny and a racial fate.

No nation can escape collective responsibility for its acceptance of the codes and policies, the ideas and actions, the standards and loyalties that bear its name.

The person who accepts doctrines, obeys commandments, follows blindly, shifts responsibility to the organization of which he or she is a member. But their attempt fails. The karma is not only collective but personal. The person as an individual cannot escape.

You have unconsciously taken a decision. It lies there, implicit, within your obedience to, and faith in, the credo or the party you follow. You are still responsible, still making personal karma.

If Alexander is to be praised for spreading Greek civilization as far east as India by the simple process of invading other countries, then the generals Flaminius, Sulla, and Mummius are to be praised for spreading Roman civilization by the simple process of invading Greece. There is a karmic connection between the two.

Great catastrophes, such as earthquakes and floods sweep hundreds to their doom, but individuals here and there escape, for their destiny is different. Such escapes often occur miraculously; they are called away suddenly to another place or protected by seemingly accidental occurrence. Thus individual destiny, where it conflicts with collective or national destiny, may save one's life where others are struck down.

History vividly shows us that at certain psychological periods unusual people arise to inspire or to instruct the age. They are men and women of destiny.

If you study history and think it over for yourself, instead of accepting the book-built theories of blind historians, you will find that the rise of great upheavals among human peoples—whether spiritual or social, military or intellectual—always synchronized with the birth and activity of great personalities.

It is nonsensical to say that a single individual *makes* a historical epoch. He or she is the embodied reaction called to play their part by the destiny of their times and by the thoughts of those among whom they are thrown.

Fate gives them unbounded faith in their own future; it forms their character and shapes their capacity to enable them to carry out an historic task in human evolution.

Karma and foreknowledge

Given a certain set of characteristics in a person, it is often possible for the psychologist to foretell in advance how that person is likely to act in a given situation.

Many events in a person's or a nation's life are foreseeable, but only if existing trends of thought and existing courses of action are continued.

Some events in the future are inevitable, either because they follow from the actions of people who fail to amend character or improve capacity or deepen knowledge, or because they follow from the basic pattern of the World-Idea and the laws it sets to govern physical life.

What will happen to each one of us in the future is not wholly inevitable and fixed, even though it is the logical sequence of our known and unknown past. It is still unset and uncrystallized—therefore changeable to a degree. That degree can be measured partly by the extent of our foreknowledge of what is likely to happen and the steps taken to circumvent it. The ability to evade these events is not a complete one, however, for it is always subject to being overruled by the will of the Overself.

I am a believer in portents. This is one weak little superstition I allow myself, that the beginning of an event carries quite an auspicious significance for me.

A warning must be given about astrological predictions. The readings must be taken with the greatest reserve. Every astrologer makes mistakes—and, frequently, tremendous mistakes—because the full knowledge of this science is lost in the modern age and there is only a partial knowledge nowadays.

There is a danger that negative predictions may also act as suggestions and, by influencing mental or emotional causes, bring about physical effects which fulfill the predictions.

The horoscope indicates the future only for ordinary people and can never become a fixed certainty for the spiritually awakened. For wherever an individual has come under Divine Grace, he or she directly or indirectly through a teacher can be rendered independent of personal past karma at any moment that the Divine wills it to be so. The will is free because Man is Divine and the Divine Self is free.

It is more important to face the future equipped with right principles and strong character than with predictions concerning its details. If we establish good attitudes toward it, we cannot get bad results.

However much we pry into the future we do not come a bit nearer real peace, whereas faithfully seeking and abiding in Overself gradually brings undying light and life.

When astrology uses the stars and planets to explain the events which happen to us as pointers to the good and evil, the wisdom and ignorance *within ourselves,* as the prime causes of these events, it serves a purpose. If, however, it uses *them* as the real causes, then it renders us a disservice.

We may freely leave the future to our stars, if we know that we can be true to ourselves.

Timing, cycles, intensity of karma

Each period of a life has its own evaluation, and opinions differ about them. Some say the early years are best, others the middle years, and so on. But the truth is that it depends on a person's karma more than on their age as to which shall prove best for them and from which they shall extract the most satisfaction.

One of the greatest misunderstandings of karma by its believers, and perhaps one of the chief hindrances to its acceptance by others, is the idea that it produces its effects only after very long periods of time. What you do today will come back to you in a future incarnation several centuries later; what you experience today is the result of what you did hundreds or even thousands of years ago; what you reap here in this twentieth century is the fruit of what you sowed there in Rome in the second century—such are the common notions about reincarnation and karma. But we have only to open our eyes and look around us to see that everywhere people are getting now the results of what they have done in this same incarnation.

Every moment we are shaping the history of the next moment, every month we are fashioning the form of the month which shall follow it. No day stands isolated and alone. Karma is a continuous process and does not work by postponement. It is indeed incorrect to regard it as a kind of post-mortem judge! But it is often not possible to work out these consequences in terms of the particular circumstances of this birth. In some cases—and in such alone—do we experience the consequences in subsequent births.

The working of karma from former lives is mostly in evidence at birth and during infancy, childhood, and adolescence. The working of karma made in the present life is mostly in evidence after the maturity of adulthood has been reached.

It is a fact in many people's lives that some of the troubles which befall them have no origin in the karma of former lives but belong solely to causes started in the present life.

It is sheer nonsense habitually to interpret karma (recompense) as something which is operative only in remote reincarnations. Actually it is mostly operative within the same lifetime of a person or nation.

There are times when the karma of an action comes back with the speed and precision of a boomerang.

It is a mistake to regard the karma of a deed as something that appears later in time, or comes back to its doer soon or long afterwards. It is not a sequence to follow after what was done before. On the contrary, the karma is simultaneous with the deed itself.

On this larger view the best karmic recompense for right actions is the upliftment of character which follows them, just as the worst karmic punishment for wrong ones is the degradation of character which is increased by them. Mentalism makes thought all-important in the end and it is so here too. For karma has a twofold character. Every deed creates both its physical reaction and the psychological tendency to repeat the deed.

We may defy the karmic law for many years in matters of the body's health and not have to pay for it until middle or old age. We may defy it in matters of conduct towards others and not have to pay until a later birth. But the law is always enforced in the end, always registered in the horoscopal chart imprinted on the very form of the body and nature of the personality.

The planets do not control your individual destiny, but their movements determine the times when the latent karma which you have earned shall become active and operative. Hence the sky is like a gigantic clock whose hands point to the fateful hours of human life but it is not a storehouse of forces influencing or dominating that life.

We hear in every religion, whether Eastern or Western, of the sufferings undergone by the wicked in the after-death state. They are supposed to dwell for a while in a nether world, a purgatory. The truth is that this is a primitive symbol of the higher doctrine that the wicked do suffer after death, but only when they are reborn on earth again.

Fate moves in rhythms of gain and loss, in cycles of accumulation and deprivation. The force which brings us loving friends and hating enemies is one and the same.

Karma waits for a proper time before calling in its accounts; its settlements being periodic and grouped together explains why good and bad fortune so often run in apparent cycles.

Quite logically it is taught that some sort of a balance

is struck between the two kinds of a person's karma, so that the bad may be mitigated or even outdone, but equally the good may be reduced or even offset.

Our inner life is fulfilled by rhythms which are under laws as much as tides and dawns are under laws.

There are so many still latent possibilities for good and evil in most people that only the turns of circumstance's wheel can develop them.

When a favorable cycle of destiny is operative, a little right action produces a lot of fortunate results. But when an unfavorable cycle is dominant, a lot of right action produces little result. The person and his or her capacities have not changed but their destiny has. At such a time, the new sequence of events in their life is dictated not by their individual will but by a higher will.

Destiny is not working blindly and unintelligently, arbitrarily and antagonistically against us as most of us are likely to believe when enduring through a cycle of unfavorable karma. On the contrary, it is Absolute Wisdom itself in operation.

The extent of the karmic consequences of an act will be proportionate to the energy it holds. The World-Mind faithfully records the loftiest aspirations or the meanest desires. If, however, the thought, emotion, or willed deed is only a passing idle one, then the impression remains dormant only and no karma is generated. Impressions which are very weak or unstrengthened by repetition are quite ineffective, but when they grow by repetition or collection they eventually become karmic and produce definite results. For this reason alone it is wisdom to nip a fault—when recognized—in the bud, and eliminate it before it becomes strong enough to do serious harm. It is also wise to remember that high ideals firmly held and lofty aspirations deeply rooted in the heart cannot fail to bear fruit of their kind in due course.

The Law is relentless but it is flexible: it adjusts punishment to a person's evolutionary grade. The sinner who knows more and who sins with more awareness of what he or she is doing, has to suffer more.

Every infraction of the great law of compensation on its moral side is cumulative, piles one eventual affliction upon another into a heap, which is one reason why we often hear the complaint that afflictions are not in just ratio with sins.

The consequences of several years of wrong doing and wrong thinking may crowd into a few months.

For some errors we have to pay with the misfortune of a few years. But for others we have to pay with the misfortune of a lifetime. An injury done to a Sage who incarnates compassion may easily, if not repented and amended, fall into the second class.

Trotsky made a point of being merciless to the enemy during Russia's Civil War: it is not surprising that his own murder was a merciless affair.

Individual accountability

Nobody has been betrayed, either by God or by life. We have contributed to, and in some measure earned, the tragic happenings of our time.

Too many people are praying to be delivered from the consequences of their errors or weaknesses, too few are trying to set themselves free from the faults themselves. If the prayers of the larger group are answered, the weaknesses still remain and the same consequences are bound to recur again. If the efforts of the smaller group are successful, they will be delivered forever.

To ascribe the results of human negligence to the operation of God's will is blasphemy. To blame the consequences of human stupidity, inertia, and indiscipline upon divine decrees is nonsense.

If people complain that life brings them its worst, they ought to pause and consider whether they have prepared themselves inwardly to receive anything better than the worst.

If you ascribe to the overwhelming nature of fate the miserable weakness of your own inertia, you worsen your bad situation.

A wiser attitude carries its outward problems into the inward realm of character, to intelligence and capacity, and deals with them there.

This blaming of others for one's misfortunes or even for one's misdeeds is, for the quester, a device whereby the ego directs attention away from its own guilt and thus maintains its hold upon the heart and the mind. For the ordinary person, it is merely the emotional expression of spiritual ignorance.

From our study of the law of karma, we may deduce that each of us must grow up, become adult, and learn to be responsible for our actions, decisions, emotions, and even thoughts. It is we who are accountable for which ideas, especially which impulses, we accept and which we let pass or push away.

3 KARMA AND GRACE

The wonder of grace

If unerring karma were the only power behind fortunes and misfortunes, it would be a sorry outlook for most of us. We have neither the knowledge, the strength, nor the virtue to accumulate much good merit. On the contrary, we have all the ignorance, the weakness, and the sinfulness to accumulate plenty of demerit. But such is the beneficence behind the universe that we are not left to the treatment of karma alone. Alongside it there exists another power, the power of grace. The two operate together, although nobody can predict how much or how little of one or the other will manifest itself in any particular case.

The view that karma operates like an automatic machine is not a wholly true one; this is because it is not a wholly complete one. The missing element is grace.

The rejection of the idea of Grace is based on a misconception of what it is, and especially on the belief that it is an arbitrary capricious gift derived from favoritism. It is, of course, nothing of the kind, but rather the coming into play of a higher law. Grace is simply the transforming power of the Overself which is ever-present but which is ordinarily and lawfully unable to act in a person until he or she clears away the obstacles to this activity. If its appearance is considered unpredictable, that is because the karmic evil tendencies which hinder this appearance vary considerably from one person to another in strength, volume, and length of life. When the karma which generated them becomes weak enough, they can no longer impede its action.

Just as this generation has lived to see the experience of gravity upset by the weightlessness experiences of spacemen, so in all the generations there have been those who have found the experience of karma upset by grace and its forgiveness.

The failure to appreciate the role of grace because of faith in the law of karma is as deplorable as the tendency to exaggerate it because of faith in a personal deity.

We need not dally idly in the stream of happenings because we believe in destiny. The Overself is deeper than destiny. The Overself is omnipotent; the related links of the chain of Fate fall to the ground at its bidding; it is worse to disbelieve in the Overself and its supremacy than to believe in destiny and its power—not that the Overself can outwit destiny, it merely dissolves it.

The Overself acts through inexorable law, yes, but love is part of the law. Grace violates no principle but rather fulfills the highest principle.

Some have difficulty in understanding the exact place in the scheme of things of Grace. If they believe in the law of recompense, there seems to be no room left for the law of Grace. It is true that we must amend our conduct and correct our faults; that no escape from these necessary duties can be found. But they can be done alone or they can be done with the thought, remembrance, and help of the Overself. This second course introduces the possibility of Grace. It can enter only if the first has been followed and only if the aspiration has succeeded in lifting the consciousness to the Overself. A moment's contact will suffice for this purpose. What happens then is that the inner change is then completed and the remaining, unfulfilled karmic consequence is then annulled. There is no giving of "something for nothing" here, no breakdown of the law of recompense. The ego must use its will to repent and amend itself, in any case.

Buddha found himself in a land where degenerate priestcraft had cunningly persuaded the masses to believe that every sin could be expiated, and its present or future effects in destiny circumvented, by some paid-for ritual, sacrifice, or magic. He tried to raise the moral level of his people by denying the pardon of sin and affirming the rigorous governance of karmic law, the strict unalterability of unseen justice. Jesus, on the contrary, found himself in a land where religion proclaimed harshly, "An eye for an eye, a tooth for a tooth." He too tried to raise the moral level of his people. But a wisdom not less than Buddha's made him meet the situation by stressing forgiveness of sins and the mercy of God. "The law of recompense brings every man his due and no external religious form can change its working" is, in effect, the gist of much Buddhist teaching. "True," Jesus might have said, "but there is also the law of love, God's love, for those who have the faith to invoke it and the will to obey it." Let us grant that both the prophets were right if we consider the different groups they were addressing, and that both gave the kind of help that was most needed by each group. Let no one deny to divinity a virtue which is possessed by humanity. The higher self's response to the ego's penitence is certain. And such response may stretch all the way to complete forgiveness of sins.

Grace is a mystical energy, an active principle pertaining to the Overself which can produce results in the fields of human thought, feeling, and flesh alike on the one hand, or in human karma circumstances and relations on the other hand. It is the cosmic will, not merely a pious wish or kindly thought, and can perform authentic miracles under its own unknown laws. Such is its dynamic potency that it can confer insight into ultimate reality as easily as it can lift a dying person back to life again or instantaneously restore the use of limbs to a crippled one.

There is hope for all because there is Grace for all. No one is so sinful that he or she cannot find forgiveness, cleansing, and renewal.

Those who believe that the universe is governed by law and that human life, as a part of it, must also be governed by law, find it hard to believe in the forgiveness of sins, and the doctrine of Grace of which it is a part. But let them consider this: that if the man fails to appropriate the lesson and to amend his conduct, if he lapses back into the old sins again, then their forgiveness automatically lapses too. The law of recompense is not negated by his forgiveness but its own working is modified by the parallel working of a higher law.

When the ego's total submission is rewarded by the Overself's holy Grace, you are granted pardon for the blackest past and your sins are truly forgiven.

There are three types of Grace: firstly, that which has the appearance of Grace but which actually descends out of past good karma and is entirely self-earned; secondly, that which a Master gives to disciples or aspirants when the proper external and internal circumstances exist—this is in the nature of a temporary glimpse only but is useful because it gives a glimpse of the goal, a sense of the right direction, and inspiring encouragement to continue on the Quest; thirdly, when a person attains the fullest degree of realization, that person is enabled in some cases to modify overhanging negative karma or in others to negate it because he or she has mastered the particular lessons that needed to be learned. This is particularly evident when the Hand of God removes obstructions in the path of their work. The philosophic conception of Grace shows it to be just and reasonable. It is indeed quite different from the orthodox religious belief about it, a belief which regards it as an arbitrary intervention by the Higher Power for the benefit of its human favorites.

The Overself does not violate the law of consequences at any time. If, through your own efforts you modify its effects upon you in a particular instance, or if the same is brought about by the manifestation of Grace, everything is still done within that law—for it must not be forgotten that the allotment selected for a particular incarnation does not exhaust the whole store of karma existing in a person's record. There is always very much more than a single earth-life's allotment. What happens is that a piece of good karma is brought into manifestation alongside of the bad karma, and of such a nature and at such a time as completely to neutralize it, if its eradication is to be the result, or partially to neutralize it, if its modification is to be the ended result. Thus the same law still continues to operate, but there is a change in the result of its operation.

The notion of grace as given out in popular religion was helpful perhaps to the masses but needs a large revision for the philosophic seekers. It is not granted at the whim of a Personal God nor solely after deserving labors for it. It is rather more like a steady permanent emanation from each person's own Overself, always available, but of which each of us must partake by ourself. If at times it seems to intervene specially on one's behalf, that is an appearance due to the immense wisdom in timing the release of a particular good karma.

Would forgiveness be an impossible nullification of the law of karma? Is there no way out of one karmic consequence leading to and creating a further one in an endless and hopeless series? I believe an answer to the first question has been given by Jesus, and to the second by Aeschylus. Matt. 12:31: "Therefore I tell you, every sin and blasphemy will be forgiven men," was Jesus' clear statement. As for the difficult problem propounded by the second question, consider the solution suggested by Aeschylus: "Only in the thought of Zeus, whatever Zeus may be." Karma must operate automatically, but the Power behind karma knows all things, controls all things, controls even karma itself, *knows and understands when forgiveness is desirable.* No human mind can fathom that Power; hence Aeschylus adds the qualifying phrase, "whatever Zeus may be." Forgiveness does not destroy the law of karma; it complements the work of that law. "All of us mortals need forgiveness. We live not as we would but as we can," wrote Menander nearly four hundred years before Jesus' time.

In the Overself we find the supreme and absolute value because it transcends the plane of ideation itself. The Overself cannot separate itself from cosmic karma but it is not subject to the working of personal causality because it is not subject to personality, change, relativity; being beyond the limits of these ideas which appear within it. When we come to examine the nature of ultimate reality we shall learn why this is so. Hence personal karma cannot operate in such a sphere of absoluteness, however rigidly and inflexibly it operates within the space-time world of relative existence. This fact that personal causation does not exist in the profoundest sense of existence offers a great hope for humanity. For it makes possible the introduction into human life and vicissitude of this totally new and unexpected factor of grace. It is like a lifebelt to which despairing mortals may cling. The worst sinner may receive what he has not earned if he will sincerely repent, make all possible amends, and turn his face around in sublime faith. Regardless of what his past life may have been if, *by change of thought and deed,* he can succeed in making his voice heard in that higher region it is always possible that there will descend this gift of grace.

There has been some questioning about the idea of Grace. It is accepted by the Christians and Hindus and denied by the Buddhists and Jains. However, even those who accept it have confused and contradictory ideas concerning it. In a broad general sense it could be defined as a benevolent change brought about without the person's own willpower, but rather by some power not commonly or normally his or her own. But because we have with us residues of former reincarnations in the form of karma, it is impossible for most persons to distinguish whether any happening is the result of karma or of Grace. But sometimes they can, for instance, if they wake up in the morning or even in the middle of the night remembering some difficulty, some situation or problem, but along with it feeling a Higher Presence and then with this feeling beginning to see light upon the difficulty or the problem and especially beginning to lose whatever distress, inquietude, fear, or uncertainty may have been caused by it. If they feel that the negative reactions vanish and a certain peace of mind replaces them, and especially if the way to act rightly in the situation becomes clear, then they are experiencing a Grace.

Intuition—which Bergson called the surest road to truth—eradicates hesitancies. When you are in contact with the Overself in solving a problem, you receive a direct command what to do and you then *know* it is right. The clouds and hesitancies and vacillations which arise when struggling between contrary points of view, melt. Whereas, if you are not in contact with the Overself, but only being carried along through karma, then you swing back and forth with emotion or opinion.

First, you must attempt to lift yourself upwards, taking the needed time and making the needed effort.

Then you will feel that some other force is lifting you gratuitously—this is the reaction, Grace.

Invoking grace

Belief in the reality of Grace and hope of its coming are excellent. But they are not to be turned into alibis for spiritual sloth and moral sin.

If the Overself's Grace does not come to your help, all your exertions will be fruitless. But, on the other hand, if you do not exert yourself, it is unlikely that the Grace will come at all.

The fact of Grace being an unpredictable descent from above does not mean that we are entirely helpless in the matter, that there is nothing we can do about it. We can at least prepare ourselves both to attract Grace and to respond aright when it does come. We can cleanse our hearts, train our minds, discipline our bodies, and foster altruistic service even now. And then every cry we send out to invoke grace will be supported and emphasized by these preparations.

If there is any law connected with grace, it is that as we give love to the Overself so do we get grace from it. But that love must be so intense, so great, that we willingly sacrifice time and thought to it in a measure which shows how much it means to us. In short, we must give more in order to receive more. And love is the best thing we can give.

The fact is that the higher power dispenses grace to all, but not all are able, willing, or ready to receive it, not all can recognize it and so many pass it by. This is why people must first work upon themselves as a preparation.

When you become acutely aware both of the sacred duty of self-improvement and of the pitiful weakness which you bring to it, the need of getting the redeeming and transforming power of Grace follows logically. You are then psychologically ready to receive it. You cannot draw Grace to himself but can only invoke and await it.

The idea of conquering your own lower nature solely by your own efforts does not allow any room for Grace. It would be better to find a more balanced approach. You need to learn in your efforts that they cannot of themselves bring all you seek. The first step to attract Grace is to humble yourself in prayer and to confess your weakness.

Grace is not a one-way operation. It is not, as a few erroneously believe, getting something free. There is nothing free anywhere. For when the Grace starts to operate it will also start to dispel those negative qualities which obstruct it. They will resist, but if you adopt the correct attitude of self-surrender and are willing to let them go, they will not be able to resist long. But if you hold on to them because they seem a part of yourself, or because they seem "natural," then either the Grace will withdraw or it will lead you into circumstances and situations that remove the obstructions forcibly, and consequently painfully.

Grace, from a source above and beyond yourself, is the last answer to all your questions, the last solvent of all your problems, when your own intellect fails with the one and your own management cannot cope with the other. And the first prayerful call for the gift must go forth by way of silencing the confusion within yourself and stilling the tumult within your mind. The ego must recognize its own natural untrustworthiness and must pause, stop its persistent activity, in passive meditation.

Two things are required of you before Grace will manifest itself in you. One is the capacity to receive it. The other is the co-operation with it. For the first, you must humble the ego; for the second, you must purify it.

Your part is to open a way, remove obstructions, gain concentration, so that the Overself's grace can reach you. The union of both activities produces the result.

If all your efforts are concentrated on self-improvement, then the circle of your thinking will be a small and limited one. The petty will become over-important in your own eyes and the insignificant will become full of meaning. It is needful to balance the one attitude with another—surrender to and faith in the power of Grace.

Those who are asking the Overself to give them its greatest blessing, its grace, should ask themselves what *they* have been willing to give the Overself—how much time, love, self-sacrifice, and self-discipline.

The conditions which help to make Grace possible include first, a simpler life than that of modern thing-ridden civilization; second, communion with, and veneration of, Nature.

Grace is wholly the operation of Overself but you may help to call it forth by your yearning and prayer, by frequently turning your gaze from your little person to this larger self. Hence no sincere and sustained cry that goes out during a crisis into the seeming void goes unheard by Overself. But it must be sincere in the sense of being uttered by your acts no less than by your thoughts. And it must be sustained in the sense of being a continuous aspiration and not merely the mood of an hour. People who sincerely invoke the higher power will not invoke it in vain, although its response may take an unexpected form sometimes not altogether to their immediate liking, sometimes far beyond their fond hopes, but always for their real rather than apparent benefit.

If you want the grace you must do something to earn it, such as attend to the wastage of time on trivial or even harmful (because negative) gossip and activities; purify your character; study the revelations of sages; reflect on the course of your life; practice mind-stilling and emotional discipline.

Those who seek grace should do something to deserve it. Let them practice forgiveness of others who have injured them; let them extend mercy to anyone in their power or needing help from them; let them stop slaughtering innocent animals. This will really be as if they were granting grace themselves. What they give to others, they may expect to receive themselves.

Grace is always being offered, in a general way, but we do not see the offer; we are blind and so pass it by. How can we reverse this condition and acquire sight? By preparing proper conditions. First, mark off a period of each day—a short period to begin with—for retreat from the ordinary out-going way of living. Give up this period to in-going, to meditation. Come out of the world for a few minutes.

Whoever invokes the Overself's Grace ought to be informed that he is also invoking a long period of self-improving toil and self-purifying affliction necessary to fit him to receive that Grace.

It is true that Grace is something which must be given from a source higher and other than yourself. But it is also true that certain efforts made by you may attract this gift sooner than it would otherwise have come. Those efforts are: constant prayer, periodical fasting.

Grace can be a ripening of karma, or a response to a direct appeal to a higher power, or can come through a saint's appeals. Faith in the Power is rewarded by grace. If the appeal fails, adverse karma must be too strong. Materialists do not make such appeals, so they receive no Grace unless the accumulation of good deeds brings good karma.

It is not possible to have the punishment of past errors remitted until we ourselves let them go by taking their lessons fully and fairly to heart.

Sorrow for a wrong course of life, the resolve to abandon it, and the readiness to make definite amendments are prerequisites to secure Grace.

Confession is a good practice when it is a sincere honest recognition that certain actions of the past were wrong actions, whether they were merely imprudent or wholly evil; that they ought never to have been committed; and that if faced by similar situations again you will try your utmost not to commit them. Remorse, penitence, and a desire to make amends are the emotional feelings which ought to accompany the intellectual recognition if it is to have effective value in the future. According to custom, there are three ways in which confession can be made. There is the way of certain religions, which enjoin the presence of an ordained priest. This is useful mainly to adherents of these religions who can bring themselves to have faith in both the dogmas and the priests. But whether done in a religious atmosphere or not, confession to another person possesses worth only if that other is really of a spiritual status superior to the sinner's own and not merely claiming or pretending it. If this safeguard is present, then confession releases the tension of secretly held sins. Secondly, there is the way of some sects and cults, which enjoin the presence of a group. This too is useful only to fellow believers, and useful in a very limited way. It offers emotional relief. But it degenerates all too easily into egoistic exhibitionism. It is certainly much less desirable than the first way. Private confession done in solitude and directed toward one's own higher Self is the third way. If the sinner experiences a feeling of being inwardly cleansed, and subsequently shows no tendency to repeat the sin, he or she may know that their confession has been effective and that the Overself's Grace has come to them in response to the act. It is a mistake to believe, however, that a single act of confession is all that is needed. It may be, but most often such response comes only as the climax of a series of such acts. It is also a mistake to believe that any confession has any value if the sinner's ego is not abjectly humiliated and made to feel not only its foolishness and unworthiness but also its dependence on the higher power for help in attaining wisdom and self-mastery.

If you try to fulfill these conditions of sincere self-preparation, and if you try to practice service, compassion, and kindliness, Grace will come and its meaning will be found. For Grace holds a significance that is very close to love, to unselfish love.

What you have given to others will be returned to you by the law of recompense.

By forgiving those who have harmed us, we put ourselves in the position of earning forgiveness for the harm we ourselves have done.

If you make yourself worthy of grace, you need not worry about whether you will ever receive it. Your earnest strivings will sooner or later merit it. And this is the best way to render its bestowal a likely happening.

You may fall into dismay at times but should never let it become despair. This helps grace to come.

Prayer is not to be scorned by anyone. We minify the power of the Overself if we do not accept this statement. So long as we are imperfect so long may we find it necessary to pray. So long as we find lack of anything so long may we have to pray. Only the sage who is integrated and desireless does not need to pray, although the sage may pray for others in his or her own mysterious unconventional way. Nor can we say it is always wrong to pray for physical things: sometimes it may be right. But a prayer which is merely a petition to a supernatural Being to remove self-earned afflictions from the petitioner and nothing more can bring no other result than the psychological comfort it gives him. It will certainly not alter by a single jot the karmic requital which is being suffered. It will merely be a noise in the air. In vain does it protest at fate. But a prayer which combines with itself the repentant effort to alter the character-defect which gives rise to the afflictions and which is the complement of an actual attempt to make reparation if someone else has been wronged, may not be a vain one. Repentance and reparation are the all-important factors which can make a prayer successful. They will then be a force which may affect personal karma because they introduce *new* and favorable karma. . . .

Let it be noted then that the God to whom we pray dwells first in our own heart. When our prayer produces an after-feeling of relief or peace, it is probably a sign that we have prayed aright, but when our perplexity or distress weighs on us as heavily as before it is probably a sign either that we must pray again and yet again or that we have prayed wrongly. In so far as a prayer exalts your thoughts above your petty personal concerns, it is sure to be helpful for your progress. In so far as it is a purely materialistic or utterly hypocritical appeal to an anthropomorphic deity to shower material benefits of a particular kind, it is sure to be useless either for spiritual or practical progress. The best way to appeal against the principle of karma when it is exacting painful tribute is not to pray but to change your thoughts. The more you can alter for the better the general trend of your thinking, the better will your external life ultimately become.

Grace is the hidden power at work along with your spirit's aspiration and your efforts at discipline. This does not mean that it will continue to work if you drop both aspiration and effort. It may, but more often it will not.

4 WORKING WITH KARMA

People will moan about their unhappy past, and ache because they cannot undo it; but they forget to undo the unhappy future which they are now busy making.

When considered from the long-range karmic point of view, each of us creates our own world and atmosphere. Therefore, we have no one but ourselves to thank or blame for our comfort or wretchedness. It should be remembered, too, that present correct or incorrect use of free will is right now deciding the conditions and circumstances of lives to come.

It is not a matter for regret when you have to face adverse circumstances, but rather a challenge as to what you can make of them. They represent a triple possibility: deterioration, stagnation, or growth. When your mind has been accustomed sufficiently long to these ideas, and when they have been recreated as the product of your own thinking and the conclusion of your own experience, they will enable you to meet the challenges of destiny and the mutations of fortune with a strength and wisdom unknown before.

When the teaching that you will inevitably receive the results of your actions wins acceptance through thoroughly satisfying the rational need of knowledge and the emotional need of justice; when this idea attains a certain degree a heartfelt force and intellectual clearness; when its innate truth is recognized as credible and its fairness as consoling, and when it begins to become dynamic in your world-outlook; it will then not only begin to exert influence on your exterior life but cannot even be stopped from influencing it. Where it apparently fails to do so, it is always either because the acceptance is merely superficial and vocal or because innate selfishness and undisciplined passion assert themselves in the subconscious character. In the first case the doctrine is known only decayed tradition or by parrot-like hearsay, as so often happens in the East. Through its conventional acceptance it has never been turned into profound conviction and consequently has lost much of its ethically disciplinary edge. In the second case the complexes are at work without a person's awareness and prevent him or her from giving full weight to the doctrine. This said, it is axiomatic that we tend to do ultimately what we think and feel.

Once a thought-series or deed is strong enough, its karmic resultant is as inevitable as a picture on an exposed photographic film. When karmic force has attained a certain impetus, its onward movement can no longer be stopped although it may be modified. This is why it is a philosophic maxim to nip undesirable growths in the bud and thus extinguish karmic energies before they become inexorably decisive. A thought which has not attained a certain fullness of growth and strength will not yield karmic consequences. The importance of nipping off wrong thoughts at the time of their arisal is thus indicated. The way to fight a bad tendency in oneself or a bad movement in a nation is to check it during the early stages before it has gathered momentum. For it is easier to scotch it at the start when it is relatively weak than later when it is relatively strong.

It is a valuable exercise for you to find out just where your own responsibility for your troubles begins, to separate what is really an outward projection of your inward defects from what is being saddled upon you by an untraceable destiny or a formidable environment.

The Pythagorean practice of nightly self-interrogation with such questions as "What have I done wrongly?" and "What duty have I left undone?" was an excellent one to counteract bad karma in the making, as was their other practice of saying and doing nothing whilst under the influence of passion.

The karma is a part of yourself and you cannot get away from it. But just as you may bring some changes about in yourself, so there may be a corresponding echo in the karma.

Only when you can judge your own fortunes with impersonality and without complaint, can you develop the capacity to understand the mystery of your destiny and why it has taken one particular course rather than another.

Karma is the precise result of what a person thinks and does. Your reaction to events and situations is the precise result of what you are, your stage in evolution. Therefore, lesser reactions and hence better fortune can come only when you elevate your evolutionary status.

Wherever you go you still take your own mind, your own heart, your own character with you. They are the real authors of your troubles. Nothing outside will change these troubles so long as you do not begin to change your psychic life, that is, yourself.

You want your exterior life unfoldment to meet your own conceptions. But if your have not found your interior harmony with God, in spite of all your efforts it will never do so.

All talismanic precautions, gem influences, and so on, either amplify or modify the other influences (karmic, environmental, and personal) which may be at work; they do not stand by themselves. More may be done in this way by changing the kind of prevailing thoughts, and especially by keeping out negative harmful and destructive thoughts, together with prayer for guidance.

Your efforts to modify the effects of evil karma (recompense) must, where you can possibly trace any of them to causes set going in the present life, include remorse for wrongs done to others, as well as for harm done to yourself. If the feeling of remorse does not come naturally at first, it may do so after several endeavors to reconsider your wrong actions from an impersonal standpoint. Constant reflection upon the major sins and errors of your past in the right way, setting the picture of your actual behavior against the picture of how you ought to have behaved, may in time generate a deep sense of sorrow and regret, whose intensity will help to purge your character and improve your conduct. If, by such frequent and impartial retrospection, the lessons of past misbehavior have been thoroughly learned, there is the further likelihood that the Overself's grace may wipe out the record of evil karma waiting to be suffered, or at least modify it.

Envy not those with good fortune. The gods have allotted them a portion of good karma, but when this is exhausted they will be stripped of many things, except those inner spiritual possessions.

Karma does not say that a person born in a slum must remain there till he or she dies. It puts them there, true; but it is up to them to get out of it by use of intelligence and personal efforts. It is true, however, that they cannot do everything they wish, for they have to start with the existing material and develop from that. "No general can be lucky unless he is bold," said General Sir Archibald Wavell. It is the same on the battlefield of life. We must be prepared to take a risk or two if we would leave the field in triumph.

Once you really take the law of consequences to heart, you will not willingly or knowingly injure another person. And this is so primarily because you will not want to injure yourself.

You have to foresee the consequences not only of an action but also of an attitude or an outlook.

If you have any grievance against another person or if you are conscious of feelings of anger, resentment, or hatred against another person, follow Jesus' advice and let not the sun go down on your wrath. This means that you must see the other person as expressing the result of all his or her own long experience and personal thinking about life and therefore the victim of their own past, not acting better only because they do not know any better. Then comprehend that whatever wrongs have been done will automatically be brought under the penalty of karmic retribution. Consequently, it is not your affair to condemn or to punish the other person, but to stand aloof and let the law of karma take care of him or her. It is your affair to understand and not to blame. You must learn to accept people just as they are, uncondemned. You certainly should try not to feel any emotional resentment or express any personal ill-will against them. You must keep your own consciousness above the evil, the wrong-doing, the weaknesses, or the faults of the other and not let them enter your own consciousness—which is what happens if you allow them to provoke negative reactions in your lower self. You should make immediate and constant effort to root such weeds out of your emotional life. But the way to do this is not by blinding yourself to the faults, the defects, and the wrongdoings of the other. Nor is it to be done by going out of your way to associate with undesirables.

Some well-meaning moralists who say that the disciple should no longer look for the evil in others, swing to the other extreme and say that we should look only for the good. Philosophy, however, does not endorse either point of view, except to remark that we have no business to judge those who are weaker than ourselves and less business to condemn them. It further says that to look only for the good in others would be to give a false picture of them, for a proper picture must combine the bright and the dark sides. Therefore it prefers mentally to leave them alone and not to set any valuation upon them, to mind its own affairs and to leave them to the unerring judgment of their own karma. The only exception to this rule is when you are forced to have dealings with another person which make it necessary for you to understand the character of the person with whom you are dealing; but even this understanding must be fair, just, calmly made, impartial, and unprejudiced. Above all, it must not arouse personal emotions or egoistic reactions: in short, you will have to be absolutely impersonal. But it is seldom that a disciple will have to make such an exception. You should refrain from giving attention to the imperfections and shortcomings of others, and you should certainly never blame them for these. You should turn your critical gaze towards yourself alone—unless you are specifically asked by others to examine them—and exercise it to correct yourself and improve yourself and reform yourself.

We need not be afraid to help others because we are afraid to interfere with their karma. Reason must guide our sympathy, it is true, and if our beneficent act is likely to involve the beneficiary in continued wrong-doing or error it may be wiser to refrain from it. It is not generosity to condone his sin and to confirm him more strongly in his foolish course. But the law of karma can be safely left to provide for its own operations. Indeed it is even possible that it seeks to use us as a channel to modify or end this particular piece of suffering in the other person. To refuse to relieve suffering, human or animal, because it may be an interference with their karma is to misapply one's knowledge of the law of karma.

Because we believe that karma operates to bring about sometimes approximate, sometimes adequate justice in the end, we must not therefore for example stand indolently aside from aggressive wrong-doing in passive trust to its operation. For karma needs to utilize instruments and its effects do not spring miraculously out of the air. Hence we must not shirk if we are called upon to cooperate with its intended educative effect, to work with its intuited operations, and to set those causes into motion through which its reactions may be produced.

The worst physical karma is created by murder. There the penalty is inescapable, however delayed. The murderer will himself be murdered, although not necessarily in the same incarnation. The worst mental karma is created by hatred. If sufficiently intense and prolonged, it will give rise to destructive diseases which eat away the flesh.

There is nothing reprehensible about holding conscientious objections to the draft for military service at a certain stage of your growth for it grows out of fine ideals. It is not a matter where anyone should attempt to dictate what you should do, for such a view is to be respected and the practice of tolerance is advisable in such an instance. Nevertheless, you should also realize that it is nothing more than a milestone from which you will one day move on. There is a higher possible view but if you cannot see its rightness or haven't the inner strength to take it, you should not worry but do whatever you think is right. And this higher view is to sink your personal feelings, to realize that having been born among the people of your country and shared its life, you have incurred a karmic responsibility to share its protection too. If their ideals are different, that does not absolve you of responsibility. Only a deliberate renunciation of citizenship and transfer of residence to another country would absolve you—and once war has been declared, it is too late. As to taking up arms and killing an enemy, if need be, here again if it is done in defense of one's country against an aggressive nation, it is not a sin but a virtue. For you are not doing it merely to protect yourself alone but others also. To that extent it is quite unselfish. Much depends on your motive. If a soldier fights selflessly as in a spirit of righteous service against a ruthless aggressor, that soldier is acting egolessly. Again, the mere killing of a physical body is not a sin but the motive which brought about that killing can alone turn it into a sin or not.

Because we hold that karma is the hidden ruler of humanity's fortunes and that force cannot be their final arbiter, we do not necessarily hold that force may therefore be dispensed with in favor of an ethic of nonviolence. . . . The sage does not accept the mystical doctrine of nonviolence for various philosophical reasons. His principal reason, however, is because he does not wish to confirm the wrong-doer in his wrong-doing, and does not wish either to smooth the latter's path and thus encourage evil, or to practice partiality towards him. A meek submission to an aggressor's will makes the aggressor believe that his methods pay, whereas a determined resistance checks his downward course, arouses doubts and even provides instruction should he suffer punishment.

The punishment of a crime without accompanying ethical education is clumsy and inefficient brutality. Prison punishment, especially, should be set in a framework of ethical instruction which includes the doctrine of karma. Without such a setting its deterrent effect is not sufficient to make it more than a half-success and a half-failure.

Counteract harmful tendencies

The unpaid mistakes and debts from former lives are now here to haunt us. If we want release from them, we must either get release from our egos or else set up counteracting thoughts and deeds of an opposite character and in overwhelming amount.

Which of us has the power to change the consequences of his or her former actions? We may make amends, we may be penitent and perform penances. We may counter them by the opposite kinds of good deeds. But it is the business of karma to make us feel responsible for what we do and that responsibility cannot be evaded. In a certain sense, however, there is a measure of freedom, a power of creativity, both of which belong to the godlike Higher Self which each of us has.

What has happened has happened and there is nothing we can do about it. We cannot rewrite the past, we cannot repair our wrong actions, we cannot put right the wrongs we have done, the hurts we have given, or the miseries we have caused both to others and to ourselves. But if the past records cannot be changed, our present attitudes towards them can be changed. We can learn lessons from the past, we can apply wisdom to it, we can try to improve ourselves and our acts, we can create new and better karma. Best of all, having done all these things, we can let go of the past entirely and learn to live in the eternal now by escaping into true Being, the I am consciousness, not the I was.

If you want to change your karma, begin by changing your attitude: first, toward outer events, people, things; second toward yourself.

To offset the karmic effects of a bad deed, do the contrary one; and of bad thought and speech we should deliberately cultivate the opposite kind. If something has been taken from a person, something should be given voluntarily which is of equal or greater value to them.

If it be true that we cannot wish our bad karma away, it is equally true that we can balance it with good karma and thus offset its results. Buddha, who was one of the greatest exponents of the karma doctrine, pointed out that right thinking and good deeds could change karmic curses into blessings.

The fixed focusing of a persistent concentrated idea will exert pressure from within, as it were, and may slowly alter your karmic physical fortunes. Karma is thought as much as action, desire as much as deed. The one is the seed which fructifies into the other and cannot be separated from it. It is this silent, secret registration in the World-Mind which makes the working of karma possible, just as the sound encoded in an audio disk make possible the hearing of its sound.

That which compels us to act in a certain way is in part the pressure of environment and in part the suggestion of our own past. Sometimes one is stronger, sometimes the other is stronger. But the root of the whole problem lies in our mind. Its proper cultivation frees us largely from both compulsions.

By watching our thought life, keeping out negatives, and cultivating positive ideas, full of trust in the higher laws, we actually start processes that eventually bring improvement to the outer life.

That which delays the expression of your dynamic thought in modifications of your environment or alterations of your character is the weight of your own past karma. But it only delays; if you keep up the pressure of concentration and purpose, your efforts must eventually show their fruit.

The more you behave with kindly qualities towards others, the more will their behavior towards you reflect back at least some of these qualities. The more you improve your own mental and moral conditions, the more will your human relations bring back some echo of this improvement.

When all malice and all envy are resolutely cast out of your nature, not only will you be the gainer by it in improved character and pleasanter karma, but also those others who would have suffered as victims of your barbed words or ugly thoughts.

The law of consequences is immutable and not whimsical but its effects may at times be modified or even neutralized by introducing new causes in the form of opposing thoughts and deeds. This of course involves in turn a sharp change in the direction of life-course. Such a change we call repentance.

Karma does not wholly cancel freedom but limits it. If the present results of old causes set walls around you, through a better character and an improved intelligence new causes may be initiated and other results be attained.

We all have to bear the consequences of our past deeds. This cannot be helped. But of course there are good deeds and bad deeds. We can, to a certain extent, offset those consequences by bringing in counter-forces through new deeds; but how far this will be true will necessarily vary from person to person. People who have knowledge and power, who are able to practice deep meditation and to control their character, will necessarily affect those consequences much more strongly than those who lack these.

The measure of this counter-influence will be the measure of the sincerity of your repentance, of the refusal to take any alibis from yourself, of the effort to change your mode of thought, and of the practical steps you voluntarily take to undo the past wrongs done to others.

What you have brought upon yourself may come to an end of itself if you find out what positive quality you need to develop in your attitude toward it to replace the negative one.

In the making of our future, a mixed result comes from the mixed and contradictory character of the thoughts feelings and desires we habitually hold. Therefore our very fears may contribute their quota in bringing about what we do not desire. Here lies one advantage of positive affirmations and clear-cut decisions in our attitude toward the future.

There are occasions when it is either prudent or wise to practice Stoic submission. But there are other occasions when it is needful to do battle with the event or the environment.

If certain evils are written in our destiny and may not be avoided by effort, it is still sometimes possible to minimize them by prudence.

You may do all you can to circumvent your destiny but although you can succeed in some particulars you cannot in others. For instance, you cannot change the color of your skin. But the kind of experiences which fall to your lot in consequence of that color are to some extent subject to your influence and character, while your own emotional reaction to them is to the fullest extent certainly subject to them.

There is no need for pessimism when your career seems to meet with insuperable obstacles and when you seem to come to an impasse which brings out nothing but a feeling of great frustration. At such times, you must remember that karma may begin to work out her own plans and that a reorientation of activities may be indicated. You should do all you can to *create* your specific opportunities and thus shorten the waiting time. The developed aspirant does not fall into conventional categories and that is why you have to strike out on a new path for yourself. It needs courage, faith, imagination, intuition, and the ability to recognize karmic opportunities and make the most of them.

You may always rightly close your prayer by soliciting guidance and sometimes by asking for forgiveness. Such a request can find justification, however, only if it is not a request for interfering with karma, only if it comes after recognition of wrong done, perception of personal weakness, confession leading to contrition, and a real effort to atone penitently and improve morally. The eternal laws of karma will not cease operating merely for the asking and cannot violate their own integrity. They are impersonal and cannot be cajoled into granting special privileges or arbitrary favors to anyone. There is no cheap and easy escape from them. If you want to avoid hurtful consequences of your own sins, you must use those very laws to help you do so, and not attempt to insult them. You must set going a series of new causes which shall produce new and pleasanter consequences that may act as an antidote to the older ones.

There is a gratifying secret entwined with the injunction to serve humankind. Whoever gives himself in such service will inevitably receive a boomerang-like return one day when others will display a readiness to serve him. For karma is a divine law which brings back to us whatever we have given forth. The area and depth of your own service will mark the area and depth of that which humankind will extend toward you. Only the form of it will be different because this will depend both on prevailing circumstances and your own subconscious or conscious desire. It may take only a mental or emotional form. The moral of this is that the wise altruist loses nothing in the end by his altruism, although the foolish altruist may lose much as the karmic consequence of his or her foolishness.

Saint Paul, following the master whom he never saw in the flesh but knew so well in the spirit, put all other virtues beneath compassion. Are the few who try to be true Christians, in this point at least, utterly wasting their time? For so say the yogis who would abolish all effort in service and concentrate on self-realization alone. Yet neither Jesus nor Paul was a mere sentimentalist. They knew the power of compassion in dissolving the ego. It was thus a part of their moral code. They knew, too, another reason why we should practice altruistic conduct and take up noble attitudes. With their help we may bring one visitation of bad karma to an earlier end or even help to prevent the manifestation of another visitation which would otherwise be inevitable.

Accept, endure, and overcome

Each of us has our own burden of bad karma. What kind and how heavy it is are important, but more important is how we carry it.

Philosophy never encourages a passive attitude towards the law of recompense, but it does not fall into the error of misleading schools of thought which hold out false hopes.

Until a certain time the course of one's destiny is within one's area of influence, and even of control; but beyond that time it is not.

It is wise to submit to the inevitable, but first it is needful to be sure that it is the inevitable. There are times when it is wiser to struggle against destiny like a captured tiger, and other times when it is wiser to sit as still in its presence as a cat by the hearth.

Resignation to circumstance, adaptation to environment, coming to terms with the inevitable, and acceptance of the unavoidable, however reluctant—these have their place as much as the use of free aggressive will.

It is the part of wisdom to learn when to attack difficulties with a bold front and when to circumvent them by patience or cunning. There is a right time for all events. If they are brought about too early, then the consequences will be a mixture of good and bad, just as if they were brought about too late. If, however, one has the patience to wait for the right moment, and the wisdom to recognize it, then the results will be unmixed good. Karma comes into play as soon as a suitable combination of factors occurs.

To strive hard for a worthwhile aim but to resign oneself to its abandonment if destiny is adverse to its realization, is not the same as to do nothing for it at all but to leave that aim entirely to fate. To eliminate within oneself the avoidable causes of misfortune and trouble but to endure understandingly those which are the unavoidable lot of human life is not the same as to let those causes remain untouched whilst blindly accepting their effects as fate.

Trying in the wrong way hinders us and trying in the right way helps us. Rebellion against fate does not help; acceptance and correction of fate does.

If you should fiercely resist karma's decrees at some times, it is also right that you should bow resignedly to them at other times. For if you have not learnt the lesson of letting go when it is wise to go, then every mistaken effort of your fingers to hold on against those decrees will only bring you further and needless pain. You should not rebel against them blindly. How to comprehend which course is to be taken is something which you have to deduce for yourself. No book can tell you this but your intuition checked by reason or your reason illumined by intuition may do so.

Such an intuition must be carefully distinguished from pseudo-intuition, which is a mere echo of your own emotional complexes, innate prejudices, or wishful thinking. The former is the authentic whisper of your own Overself. The ageless Overself holds all the innumerable memories of its related personalities in solution, as it were, so that they are and yet are not. It wills only what is karmically earned by you during these successive lives, which is always what will justly compensate you for the characteristics you have manifested though your actions. And because the Overself is the source of this karmic adjustment, it may be said that each of us is truly our own judge. For it must never be forgotten that fundamentally the Overself is one's own central self; it is not something alien or remote from you.

What is the use of fooling oneself with stirring phrases about our freedom to mold life or with resounding sentences about our capacity to create fortune? The fact remains that karma holds us in its grip, that the past hems us in all around, and that the older we grow the smaller becomes the area of what little freedom is left. Let us certainly do all we can to shape the future and amend the past, but let us also be resigned to reflective endurance of so much that will come to us or remain with us, do what we may.

Such an enlightened and qualified fatalism need not lead to a paralysis of the will and passivity of the brain. It emphatically does not lament that we can do nothing to change our lot for the better nor, worse, leave us without even the desire to change it. No—the submission to fate which a doctrine teaches is not less enlightened and qualified than itself. Its effect upon those who not only believe in it but also understand it, is towards the striking of a balance between humble resignation and determined resistance, towards the correct appraisal of all situations so that the truly inevitable and the personally alterable are seen for what they are. It yields to God's will but does not therefore deny the existence of our own.

We may take defeat in a spirit of bitter resentment or melancholy pessimism. Both these attitudes are wholly unprofitable. There is a third and better way—to make defeat serve as the starting point of a different advance. This can be done by, first, a frank ungrudging and searching self-examination to discover faults and confess wrongs, and second, by deeds of repentant amends and the pioneering of a new outlook.

If karmic obligations may have to be fulfilled, at least this will not be done in total ignorance. It will be with resignation rather than hatred, and with hope for higher attainment.

You may have to learn how to accommodate what you cannot control or avoid. This is resignation, the very name—Islam—of the religion given to the world by Muhammed. But if you have to accept certain things, this is not to say that their accommodation implies his approval of them. It means rather that you cease to grumble or worry about them.

Even if your intuitive feeling warns you of an impending event in such a manner that you know it to be unalterably preordained and inevitable, your inability to prevent it from happening need not prevent you from making all possible preparations to protect yourself and thus to suffer less from it than you might otherwise have done. Such a warning can only be useful and saves you from falling into the panic in which fear of the unexpected may throw others.

Now and then karma unloads trials and troubles which are not pleasant to endure. All the same they have something to teach us—if only the ancient lesson of the need to find a more satisfactory inner life to compensate for the transiency and the vicissitudes of the outer life. You cannot escape from these so long as you live upon this earth but you can hope to understand them and eventually to master your mental reactions to them. Therein lies peace and wisdom.

There is always some part of our person or fortune which remains wholly beyond our control. Do what we will we cannot alter it. It is then more prudent to acknowledge the inevitability of this condition than to waste strength in useless struggle. Sometimes you may then even turn it to your advantage. But how are you to know that this inevitability, this decree of fate, exists? By the fact that no matter how much you exert yourself to alter it, you fail.

Internally and externally, we find through experience that a certain arc of fate has been drawn for us and must consummate itself. Futile is the endeavor to try to cross that arc; wise is the submissiveness that stays within its limits. We must leave to it the major direction which our mental and physical life must take. The thoughts that shall most move us and the events that shall chiefly happen to us are already marked on the lines of the arc. There is nothing arbitrary, however, about this, for the thoughts and the events are related and both together are still further related to an interior birth in the long series that makes up human life on this planet.

If this is the way your life has to be, if this is how the cards of your destiny have fallen, and if the inner voice bids you accept it after the outer voice has led you into unavailing attempts to alter it, then there must be some definite reason for the situation. Search for this reason.

Accept fully and without demur your self-made karma, even to the extent of refraining from asking to be forgiven your sins, for it is a just result. Ask instead to be shown how to overcome the weakness which had been the cause.

When you accept affliction as having some message in it which you must learn, you will be able to bear it with dignity rather than with embitterment.

We must learn to let go, to renounce voluntarily that which destiny is determined to take away from us. Such an acceptance is the only way to find peace and the only effective path to lasting happiness. We must cease to regard our individual possessions and relationships as set for all time.

There are forces which predetermine our destiny and we must know when to win battles—like Napoleon—by retreating, by submitting to Fate's decree. In the last chapter of *The Hidden Teaching Beyond Yoga,* a technique used by expert boxers was recommended as supplying an excellent principle wherewith to meet the unavoidable blows of a bad karmic cycle. Another illustration of this point which will be helpful is ju-jitsu, whose principle is to conquer an adversary by giving way to him in so skillful a manner that he is forced to use his own strength either to defeat himself or to injure his own muscles. So we may conquer unalterable bad karma by yielding to it for a time but finally drawing from it such wisdom and reaction that we rise higher than before.

When you have made this surrender, done what you could as a human being about it and turned the results over completely to the higher self, analyzed its lessons repeatedly and taken them deeply to heart, the problem is no longer your own. You are set free from it, mentally released from its karma, whatever the situation may be physically. You know now that whatever happens will happen for the best.

A grievous marriage situation may itself change completely for the better or else a second marriage may prove a happier one, if there is sufficient improvement in thinking to affect the karma involved.

You will not be karmically free of an unpleasant relationship until you have mentally freed yourself from all negative thoughts and negative acts concerning it. Then the outer karmic forces will free you, or else you may be shown inwardly how to free yourself outwardly.

It is not necessary that you remain married in order to pay a karmic debt, nor on the other hand are you free to follow personal desires in the matter. It is a mistake to think that such a debt must continue to be paid until the end of one's life. Yet, it must be paid off if one's inner life and path are not to be obstructed. Only the voice of your own deeper conscience may decide this point.

The situations peculiar to family life not infrequently bring together two souls whose karmic relation is not that of love but of enmity. They may be brought together as brother and sister, or even as husband and wife. What should be the philosophical attitude of one to the other? Taking a concrete example and assuming the case of marital discord, and without prejudice to the practical methods such as separation or divorce—which may be considered necessary—it may be said that the enlightened partner should regard the other first as a revealing agent to bring his or her own faults into sharp definition, and second as a laboratory wherein he or she can experiment with the eradication of such faults. Thus if the wife frequently flares into passionate anger, or constantly expresses nagging abuse, her provocations ought not to be allowed to call forth the husband's anger but rather his latent self-control; her lack of considerateness should arouse not a corresponding lack on his part but rather more considerateness. In this way the situation provoked by her conduct can be converted into an opportunity to rise to higher things. Every domestic quarrel, however petty, should enable him to show forth something of the diviner aspects within himself. Again even assuming the two are radically unsuited to each other and sooner or later will have to part, the unhappiness thereby caused should be used by the enlightened partner to make him or her more determined to gain independence from external things for happiness, and to become more reliant upon those inner satisfactions which only the best in the mind can yield. Furthermore, they should make the person understand that he or she is expiating past karma which is self-earned through his or her own impulsiveness, stupidity, or passion.

5 KARMA AND THE GREAT LIBERATION

The privileges of enlightenment can only be justified on the basis of karma—"My own, my own, shall come to me," as the poet intuited.

Just as we have to look at the world in the twofold way of its immediate and ultimate understanding, so we have to find enlightenment in a twofold way through our own self-creative efforts and through the reception of Grace.

No one is excluded from that first touch of Grace which puts them upon the Quest. All may receive it and, in the end, all do. But we see everywhere around us the abundant evidence that a person will not be ready for it until he or she has had enough experience of the world, enough frustration and disappointment to make them pause and to make them humbler.

To come into the consciousness of the Overself is an event which can happen only by grace. Yet there is a relation between it and the effort which preceded it, even though it is not an exact, definite, and universally valid relation.

Aspirants who depend solely on their own unaided efforts at self-improvement will nevertheless one day feel the need of an outside power to bestow what they cannot get by themselves. The task they have undertaken cannot be perfectly done or completely done by themselves alone. They will eventually have to go down on their knees and beg for Grace. The ego cannot save itself. Why? Because secretly it does not want to do so, for that would mean its own extinction. So unless you force it to seek for Grace, all your endeavors will bring you only a partial result, never a fully satisfactory one. Those who say that the idea of Grace violates the concept of universal law do not look into it deeply enough. For then they would see that, on the contrary, it fulfills the law of the individual mind's effort, which they believe in, by complementing it with the law of the Universal Mind's activity inside the individual, which they ought also to believe in. God cannot be separated from humanity. The latter does not live in a vacuum.

The destiny of the ego is to be lifted up into the

Overself, and there end itself or, more correctly, transcend itself. But because it will not willingly bring its own life to a cessation, some power from outside must intervene to effect the lifting up. That power is Grace and this is the reason why the appearance of Grace is imperative. Despite all its aspirations and prayers, its protestations and self-accusations, the ego does not want the final ascension.

Constant self-effort can thin down the egoism but not eliminate it. That final act is impossible because the ego will not willingly slay itself. What self-effort does is to prepare the way for the further force which can slay it and thus makes the operation timely and its success possible. What it further does is to improve intelligence and intuition and to ameliorate the character, which also prepares the individual and attracts those forces. They are nothing else than the pardoning, healing, and, especially, the transforming powers of Grace.

How can the ego's self-effort bring about the grand illumination? It can only clear the way for it, cleanse the vehicle of it, and remove the weaknesses that shut it out. But the light of wisdom is a property of the innermost being—the Soul—and therefore this alone can bring it to you. How can the ego give or attain something which belongs to the Overself? It cannot. Only the divine can give the divine. That is to say, only by grace can illumination be attained, no matter how ardently you labor for it.

When your efforts have brought you to a certain point, then only do they get pushed aside or slowly drawn away by another power—your higher Self. What really happens is that the energy or power which you are using spontaneously ignites. It is that which enables you to do, to get done, to achieve. The all-important point is that the active power is not your own will, but is really a direct visitation of what we must call Grace. It is strongly felt, this experience of the higher power or higher Self.

The spiritual inertia which keeps most people uninterested in the quest is something which they will not seek to overcome by their own initiative. Life therefore must do this for them. Its chief method is to afflict them with pain, loss, disappointment, sickness, and death. But such afflictions are under karma and not arbitrary, are intermittent and not continuous, are inlaid with joys and not overwhelming. Therefore their result is slow to appear.

In certain cases where one destined for great advancement on the spiritual path willfully refuses to enter upon it or impatiently postpones such entrance for a later period, the Overself will often take a hand in the game and release karma of frustrated ambitions, disappointed hopes, and even broken health. Then in despair, agony, or pain, the wayfarer will drink the cup of voluntary renunciation or wear the shabby clothes of self-denial. His ego diminishes its strength out of suffering. His real enemy on the path is the 'I', for it is the cause of both material suffering and mental anguish, whilst it blocks the gate to truth. The more the course of worldly events depresses him, the more he will learn to withdraw from his depression into the forgetfulness of spiritual contemplation. It is enough for a votary of mysticism to find temporary peace in this way; but for a votary of philosophical mysticism, it is not. Such a one must insert reflection upon the meaning of those events into his contemplation. When he has attained to this impersonal insight, he may look back upon his past life and understand why so much of what happened had to happen.

Beyond personal karma

The working of your karma would never come to an end if your egoism never came to an end. It would be a vicious circle from which there would be no escape. But when the sense of personal selfhood, which is its cause and core, is abandoned, the unfulfilled karma is abandoned too.

There are two kinds of immortality (so long as the lower self dominates consciousness): first, the "endless" evolution of the ego, gradually developing through all its many manifestations; and, secondly, the true immortality of the everlasting, unchanging Real Self—or Overself—which forever underlies and sustains the former.

My reference to not clinging to the ego simply means that we must learn the art of releasing what is transitory in ourself and in our existence—that which can survive only temporarily. The Real Individuality—the sense and feeling of simply Being—can never perish, and is the true immortality. No one is asked to sacrifice all interest and appreciation in "things": one may continue to appreciate them—provided their transiency is understood and one does not deceive oneself into overvaluing them. The prophets merely say that the eternal life cannot be found in such things.

Where is the hope for humanity if there is no Grace, only karma? If it took so many ages to collect the karmic burden we now carry, then it will take a similar period to disengage from it—the forbidding task will continue throughout every reincarnation until each of us dies again and again—unless the individual collector, the ego, is no longer here to claim it. But to cancel its own existence is impossible by its own efforts, yet possible by its non-effort, its surrender, its letting in the Higher Power, by no longer claiming its personal identity. The coming in, when actualized, *is* Grace for it is not our doing.

The ultimate secret of Grace has never been solved by those who do not know that previous reincarnations contribute to it. Some people receive it only after years of burning aspiration and toil but others, like Francis of Assisi, receive it while unprepared and unaspiring. Ordinary candidates cannot afford to take any chance in this matter, cannot risk wasting a lifetime waiting for the unlikely visitation of Grace. They had better offer their all, dedicate their life, and surrender their loves to one all-consuming passion for the Overself, if they want the power of Grace to flow into them. If they are unable to give themselves so totally, let them do the next best thing, which is to find someone who has him or herself been granted the divine Grace and who has become inwardly transformed by it. Let them become such a person's disciple, and they will then have a better chance of Grace descending on them than they would have had if they walked alone.

The yearning to free yourself from the limitations of personal destiny and the compulsions of outward circumstance can be gratified only by losing the sense of time.

There are great dangers in falling into a supine attitude of *supposed* submission of our will, an attitude into which so many mystics and religionists often fall. There is a profound difference between the pseudo-surrendered life and the genuine surrendered life. It is easy enough to misinterpret the saying "Thy will be done." Jesus, by his own example, gave this phrase a firm and positive meaning. Hence this is better understood as meaning "Thy will be done *by me.*" A wide experience has revealed how many are those who have degenerated into a degrading fatalism under the illusion that they were thereby cooperating with the will of God; how many are those who have, through their own stupidity, negligence, weakness, and wrong-doing, made no effort to remedy the consequences of their own acts and thus have had to bear the suffering involved to the full; how many are those who have failed to seize the opportunity presented by these sufferings to recognize that they arose out of their own defects or faults and to examine themselves in time to become aware of them and thus avoid making the same mistake twice. The importance of heeding this counsel is immense. For example, many aspirants have felt that fate has compelled them to work at useless tasks amid uncongenial surroundings, but when their philosophic understanding matures, they begin to see what was before invisible—the inner karmic significance of these tasks, the ultimate educative or punitive meaning of those environments. Once this is done they may rightly, and should for their own self-respect, set to work to free themselves from them. Every time you patiently crush a wrong or foolish thought, you add to his inner strength. Every time you bravely face up to a misfortune with calm impersonal appraisal of its lesson, you add to your inner wisdom. The person who has thus wisely and self-critically surrendered may then go forward with a sense of outward security and inward assurance, hopeful and unafraid, because he or she is now aware of the benign protection of their Overself. If you have taken the trouble to understand intelligently the educative or punitive lessons they hold for you, you may then—and only then—conquer the evils of life, if at the same time of their onset, you turn inward at once and persistently realize that the divinity within offers you refuge and harmony. This twofold process is always needful and the failures of Christian Science are partially the consequence of its failure to comprehend this.

By this grace the past's errors may be forgotten so that the present's healing may be accepted. In the joy of this grace, the misery of old mistakes may be banished forever. Do not return to the past—live only in the eternal Now—in its peace, love, wisdom, and strength.

If you come into alignment with the Overself-consciousness, you are compelled to give up your earlier position of free will and free choice—for you no longer exist to please the ego alone. The regulating factor is now the Overself itself.

Your innate tendencies may still be there for a time—they constitute your karma—but the grace keeps them in check.

Whoever acts by becoming so pliable as to let the Overself hold his personal will, must necessarily become inwardly detached from the personal consequences of his deeds. This will be true whether those consequences be pleasant or unpleasant. Such detachment liberates him from the power of karma, which can no longer catch him in its web, for "he" is not there. His emotional consciousness preceding an action is always enlightened and characterized by sublime composure, whereas the unenlightened person's may be characterized by motivations of self-centered desire, ambition, fear, hope, greed, passion, dislike, or even hate—all of which are karma-making.

Mental peace can come only by paying the price for it, and part of that price is the freeing of oneself from over-dependence on externals. The mind must be freed from worry and anxiety instead of yielding in hopeless submission to them. This will invoke and assist the protective forces. All bitter thoughts towards other individuals must be banished. Love must be given whether or not it is returned, and given equally to the weak and the strong. A rich inner compensation awaits those who can endure in this way.

Karma comes into play only if the karmic impression is strong enough to survive. In the case of the sage, because he treats life like a dream, because he sees through it as appearance, all his experiences are on the surface only. His deep inner mind remains untouched by them. Therefore he makes no karma from them, therefore he is able when passing out of the body at death to be finished with the round of birth and death forever.

If you can act attentively and yet stand aside from the results of your actions; if you can discharge your responsibilities or carry out your duties without being swept into elation by success or into misery by failure; if you can move in the world, enjoy its pleasures and endure its pains, and yet hold unwaveringly to the quest of what transcends the world, then you have become what the Indians call a "karma yogi" and what the Greeks call a "man."

With the significance of your sufferings properly understood and the needful adjustments in action, character, or intelligence properly made, you may seek and keep that mental equilibrium which is inner peace. In making these truths your own you will face the hardships of life with fortitude and the inevitability of death with serenity. Thus you can learn to move with an undaunted heart amid earthly troubles and with an unruffled mind amid earthly joys not because you seek ostrich-like to forget the one and reject the other but because you seek sage-like to understand them. For in the words of a Mongolian text, "Whoso bears joy and sorrow with even mind has spirituality, although he may outwardly seem a worldling."

It would be easy to mistake such a serenity either for mere smugness or for shallow optimism. It cannot be the first because it is too conscious both of the defects of its possessor and the miseries of mankind. It cannot be the second because it is born of truth, not of emotional self-deception. It is a quality which emerges after long philosophical practice. It smiles only because it understands, not because it is emotionally basking in the rays of temporary good fortune.

Nobody succeeds in extinguishing karma merely because he intellectually denies its existence, as the votaries of some cults do. If, however, they first faced up to their karma, dealt with it and used it for self-cultivation and self-development, and then only recognized its illusoriness from the ultimate standpoint, their attitude would be a correct one. Indeed, their attempt to deny karma prematurely shows a disposition to rebel against the divine wisdom, a short-sighted and selfish seeking of momentary convenience at the cost of permanent neglect of the duty to grow spiritually.

Do your best to mend matters, the best you can, then leave the results to destiny and the Overself. You can't do more anyway. You can modify your destiny, but certain events are unchangeable because the world is not yours but God's. You may not know at first what events these are, therefore you must act intelligently and intuitively: later you can find out and accept. Whatever happens, the Overself is still there and will bring you through and out of your troubles. Whatever happens to your material affairs happens to your body, not the real YOU. The hardest part is when you have others dependent on you. Even then you must learn how to commend them to the kindly care of the Overself, and not try to carry all the burden on your own shoulders. If it can take care of you, it can take care of them, too.